Great Ideas of Science

ISAAC ASIMOV

Illustrated by Lee Ames

1969
HOUGHTON MIFFLIN COMPANY BOSTON

To Eric Berger

who has always been cooperative

FIRST PRINTING   R

COPYRIGHT © 1969 BY ISAAC ASIMOV
ALL RIGHTS RESERVED. NO PART OF THIS WORK MAY
BE REPRODUCED OR TRANSMITTED IN ANY FORM BY ANY
MEANS, ELECTRONIC OR MECHANICAL, INCLUDING PHOTOCOPYING
AND RECORDING, OR BY ANY INFORMATION STORAGE OR RETRIEVAL
SYSTEM, WITHOUT PERMISSION IN WRITING FROM THE PUBLISHER.
LIBRARY OF CONGRESS CATALOG CARD NUMBER 70-82476
PRINTED IN THE U.S.A.

5909

CONTENTS

1

Thales and Science Itself

WHAT IS the universe composed of?

About 600 B.C. the Greek thinker Thales (THAY-leez) asked himself that important question and came up with the *wrong* answer: "All things are water."

This statement was not only incorrect, it was not even quite original. Yet it is one of the most important statements in the history of science. Without it — or something like it — there would be no science.

The importance of Thales' answer will become clear if we first examine how he happened to hit upon it. Not surprisingly, this man who said that all things were water lived in a seaport. The city, Miletus (migh-LEE-tus), lay on the eastern coast of the Aegean Sea, in what is now part of Turkey. Miletus no longer exists, but in 600 B.C. it was the most prosperous city in the Greek-speaking world.

On Ancient Shores

Perhaps Thales pondered the nature of the universe at the seashore, as he gazed at the Aegean. He knew that the Aegean opened southward into a still larger sea, now called the Mediterranean, which stretched hundreds of miles westward. The Mediterranean passed through a narrow strait (the Strait of Gibraltar) between two rocky prominences the Greeks called the Pillars of Hercules.

Beyond the Pillars of Hercules lay an ocean (the Atlantic), and the Greeks thought it surrounded the world's land on all sides. Thales thought that the land was shaped like a disk a few thousand miles across and that it floated in an endless ocean.

But he knew even the land itself was riddled with water. Rivers crossed it, lakes dotted it, springs welled up from beneath. Water dried up and disappeared into the air, occasionally turning back into water and falling as rain. There was water above, water below, water on all sides.

Land Made of Water?

The very solids of the land, so it seemed to Thales, were formed from water. Thales thought he had seen this happen with his own eyes in his youth. While traveling in Egypt he had seen the Nile River rise in a flood that spread out over the land. When the waters receded, fresh fertile soil was left behind.

Indeed, in the north of Egypt where the Nile River met the sea, there was an area of deep, soft soil that had been formed by the flood waters. (It was triangular in shape, like the letter "delta" of the Greek alphabet. For this reason the region was called the Nile Delta.)

Having thought of all this, Thales came to what seemed to him to be a logical conclusion: "All things are water." Of course, he was wrong, for not all things are water. Air is not water, and while water vapor may mingle with air, it does not become air. Solid earth is not water. Particles of earth may be carried by rivers from the mountains to the plains, but those particles are not made of water.

Thales *vs.* Babylon

Thales' idea was not quite his own. It originated in Babylonia, another country he had visited as a young man. The ancient civilization of Babylonia had reached certain important conclusions about astronomy and mathematics that must have fascinated a serious thinker such as Thales. The Babylonians considered the solid land to be a disk set in a pit of fresh water. This water rose to the surface here and there to form rivers, lakes, and springs. All around the land was salt water.

But isn't this the same picture presented by Thales? Wasn't Thales just repeating Babylonian theories?

Not quite! Unlike Thales the Babylonians did not think of water as water, but as a collection of supernatural beings. The fresh water was the god Apsu, while the salt water was the goddess Tiamat. Together they gave birth to a large number of other gods and goddesses. (The Greeks had a similar notion: they thought the god of the ocean, Okeanos, was the father of the gods.)

Eventually, according to Babylonian mythology, there was war between Tiamat and her descendants. After a gigantic battle one of the new gods, Marduk, killed Tiamat and split her in two. With one half of Tiamat he made the sky and with the other half, the solid earth.

That was the Babylonian answer to the question, "Of

what is the universe composed?" Thales approached the same answer from a different angle. His picture of the universe was different because it did without gods and goddesses and without great battles between supernatural beings. He simply said, "All things are water."

Thales had pupils in his own city of Miletus and in neighboring communities on the Aegean shore. Twelve cities on this shore made a region called Ionia. Thus, Thales and his pupils are known as the "Ionian school."

The Ionians continued to try to explain the universe without resorting to gods and goddesses. In this way they established a tradition that has lasted down to the present day.

Importance of the Ionian Tradition

Why was it so important to interpret the universe without falling back on deities? Could science have developed without such a tradition?

Suppose a universe is made by gods and controlled by them. Then, they can do as they wish with the universe. If some goddess is angry because the temple built to her is not large enough, she might send a plague. If some warrior is in a bad spot and prays to a god, promising to sacrifice cattle to him, that god may send a cloud to hide him from his enemies. One cannot count on the universe's behaving in any certain way: Everything depends on the whim of some deity.

In the view of Thales and his pupils, however, no deities interfered with the workings of the universe. The universe behaved only in accordance with its own nature. Plagues arose and clouds appeared only out of certain natural causes. *Only* if those natural causes existed, would a plague arise or a cloud appear. Thus, Thales and his followers had arrived at a basic assumption: *The universe behaves in accordance with certain "laws of nature" that cannot be altered or changed.*

Is such a universe better than one that behaves according to the whims of the gods? If the deities do as they please, who can foretell what might happen tomorrow? Even the sun might not rise if the "sun god" were annoyed about something. Men who had their minds fixed on the supernatural could see no point in trying to figure out the workings of the universe. Instead, they would rather devise methods for pleasing the gods or for soothing them when they grew angry. It would be more important to build temples and altars, to work out methods of sacrifice and special prayers, to mold idols and make magic.

Nor could anything prove this system to be wrong. Suppose there was a drought or a plague despite all the ritual. This would mean only that the medicine men had done something improper or left something out. They would simply have to try again, sacrifice more cattle, and pray more carefully.

But if the basic assumption of Thales and his pupils was right — if the universe did work according to laws of nature that did not change — then it *was* worthwhile to study the universe. One could observe how the stars moved, the clouds drifted, the rains fell, the plants grew. One could be certain that those observations would hold good always and would never change suddenly because of some god. One could then work out a set of simple laws describing the general nature of the observations.

Thus, the first assumption of Thales and his followers led to a second: *It is possible for human reason to work out the nature of the laws governing the universe.*

Idea of Science

These two assumptions, that there are laws of nature and that man can work them out by reason, make up the "idea of science." Mind you, these assumptions are just assumptions; they cannot be proved. Nevertheless, since Thales there have always been men who clung firmly to belief in them.

The idea of science nearly faded out in Europe after the fall of the Roman Empire — but not quite. In the sixteenth century the idea suddenly began to grow strong. Now, in the last half of the twentieth century, it is at a peak of power.

To be sure, the universe is far more complex than Thales could possibly have imagined. Still, some laws of nature can be expressed very simply and are, as far as we now know, unshakable. Perhaps the most important of these is the "law of conservation of energy," which, stated simply, is: "The total energy of the universe is constant."

The Certain Uncertain

Science has learned there are limits to knowledge, too. In the 1920's a German physicist, Werner Heisenberg, worked out the "principle of uncertainty." He stated that it was impossible to determine precisely both the position and velocity of an object at a particular instant of time. We can determine one or the other as precisely as we please, but not both at the same time. Does this mean that the second assumption of science is wrong? That man cannot gather knowledge with which to reason out the riddle of the universe?

No, not at all, for the principle of uncertainty is itself a natural law. There are limits to the exactness with which we can measure the universe, yes, but the extent of those limits can be worked out by reason. Indeed, through proper understanding of uncertainty, much more can be learned about the universe that would be puzzling without that understanding. Thus, Thales' great "idea of science" holds as well now as it did when he advanced it some twenty-five hundred years ago.

2

Pythagoras and Number

NOT LONG AFTER the time that Thales was pondering the mysteries of the universe, around twenty-five hundred years ago, another Greek scholar was playing with strings. Like Thales (see Chapter 1), the scholar Pythagoras (pih-THAG-oh-ras) lived in a coastal city — the city of Croton, in southern Italy. Like Thales, Pythagoras was no ordinary man.

And his "playthings" were no ordinary strings, but tough cords like those used in such musical instruments as the lyre. Pythagoras had prepared cords of different lengths, held them taut, and plucked each one to produce a musical note.

Musical Numbers

Finally, he found two cords that sounded notes just an octave apart. That is, one sounded low *do* (pronounced "doe"), the other high *do*. What fascinated Pythagoras was that the cord producing low *do* was exactly twice as long as the one producing high *do*. The ratio of lengths of the two cords was 2 to 1.

He tried again and obtained two cords which sounded notes that made up a "fifth." That is, one note was *do* and the other *sol*. This time the cord producing the lower note was just one and a half times as long as the cord producing the higher one. The ratio of lengths was 3 to 2.

If one cord was one and a third times as long as another, a "fourth" was produced. That is, one note was *do* and the other was *fa*. Here the ratio of lengths was 4 to 3.

Certainly, musicians in Greece and in other lands also knew how to prepare cords that sounded certain notes and how to make them into musical instruments. Pythagoras, however, was the first man known to ponder not over the music, but over the ratio of lengths that produced the music.

Why should these ratios of small numbers — 2 to 1, 3 to 2, 4 to 3 — produce especially agreeable sounds? If Pythagoras took two cords of more complicated ratios of length, say 23 to 13, the sound combination was unpleasant.

Perhaps at this point Pythagoras snapped his fingers. Numbers were not merely tools for counting and measuring; they controlled music and perhaps they controlled all the universe.

If numbers were so important, then it became important to study them for their own sake. For example, one had to begin by thinking of the number 2 itself, not of two men or two apples or two stars. The number 2 could be evenly divided by 2; it was an *even number*. The number 3 could not be evenly divided by 2; it was an *odd number*. Now what properties did all even numbers have in common? What about all odd numbers? One could start with the fact that the sum of two even numbers or of two odd numbers is always an even number. And the sum of an even number and an odd number is always an odd number.

Or suppose one drew each number as dots. For 6, one drew six dots; for 23, twenty-three dots, and so on. If one spaced the dots equally, he would find that some numbers, known as *triangular numbers*, could be made to form orderly triangles. Others, known as *square numbers*, could become neat squares.

Triangular Numbers

Pythagoras knew that only certain numbers of dots could be made to fit into a triangle, which is a three-sided figure. The smallest was *one* dot, representing the triangular number 1.

Larger triangles could be made by placing additional lines of dots parallel to a side of a smaller triangle. For example, a three-dot triangle, representing the number 3, could be made by placing *two* dots next to a side of the one-dot triangle. Similarly, a six-dot triangle, representing the number 6, was formed by adding *three* dots to the three-dot triangle.

The next triangles in the series were made up of ten dots (the six-dot triangle plus *four* dots), fifteen dots (ten dots plus *five*), twenty-one dots (fifteen dots plus *six*), and so on. Thus, the series of triangular numbers was 1, 3, 6, 10, 15, 21, . . .

As Pythagoras built up the series of triangles by adding dots, he became aware of an interesting fact. As he moved from smaller to large triangles, the number of dots that

had to be added kept increasing by one. (You can verify
this by looking for the italicized words in the previous
three paragraphs.)

In other words, he could build up the triangles, or triangular numbers, by a series of sums of consecutive numbers. Thus, $1=1$; $3=1+2$; $6=1+2+3$; $10=1+2+3+4$;
$15=1+2+3+4+5$; $21=1+2+3+4+5+6$; and so on.

Square Numbers

Unlike the three-sided triangle, the square had four sides
(and four right, or 90-degree, angles). Therefore, Pythagoras could expect the series of square numbers to turn
out to be quite different from the triangular series. However, *one* isolated dot would fit into a square as easily as
into a triangle. Thus, the square series, too, began with
the number 1.

Larger squares were built up by placing additional dots
around two adjacent sides of another square. The new
dots were spaced along two lines that formed a right angle.
For example, *three* dots were added to the one-dot square
to form a four-dot square, which represented the number
4. A nine-dot square was made similarly, by placing *five*
dots around the four-dot square.

The series continued with squares of sixteen dots (the

nine-dot square plus *seven* dots), twenty-five dots (sixteen dots plus *nine*), thirty-six dots (twenty-five dots plus *eleven*), and so on. The outcome was the series of square numbers: 1, 4, 9, 16, 25, 36, . . .

Since the triangles had grown larger in a regular way, Pythagoras was not surprised to see the squares behaving similarly. The number of dots added to each new square was always an odd number. And it was always two dots greater than the number added to the previous square. (See the italicized words in the previous paragraphs.)

In other words, square numbers could be built up by a series of sums of consecutive *odd* numbers. Thus, $1=1$; $4=1+3$; $9=1+3+5$; $16=1+3+5+7$; $25=1+3+5+7+9$; and so on.

Squares could also be made by adding two consecutive triangular numbers: $4=1+3$; $9=3+6$; $16=6+10$; $25=10+15$; . . . Or by multiplying a number by itself: $1=1\times1$; $4=2\times2$; $9=3\times3$; . . .

The last method is a particularly important way of forming square numbers. Since $9=3\times3$, we say that 9 is the square of 3. In the same way, 16 is the square of 4, 25 is the square of 5, and so on. On the other hand, we say that the smaller number — that is, the one we multiplied by itself — is the square root of its product. For example, 3 is the square root of 9, and 4 is the square root of 16.

Right Triangles

Pythagoras' interest in square numbers led him to consider *right triangles* — triangles in which one angle is a
right angle. A right angle has two perpendicular sides —
that is, if one of the sides is held perfectly horizontal, the
other will be perfectly vertical. A right triangle adds a
third side which runs from one side of the right angle to
the other. This third side, called the "hypotenuse," is
always longer than either of the other sides.

Suppose Pythagoras drew a right triangle at random and
measured the lengths of the sides. If he divided one side
into a whole number of units, the other two sides usually
did not consist of whole numbers of the same units.

There were exceptions, though. Suppose he had a right
triangle in which one side was just three units long, and
the other just four units long. It turned out that the hypotenuse would then be exactly five units long.

Why should the numbers 3, 4, and 5 make up a right
triangle? The numbers 1, 2, 3 did not, nor did the numbers
2, 3, 4, nor almost any other combination.

Suppose Pythagoras considered the squares of the numbers. Instead of 3, 4, 5, he now had 9, 16, 25. Now something interesting showed up, for $9+16=25$. The sum of
the squares of the sides of this particular right triangle was
equal to the square of the hypotenuse.

Pythagoras went further. He noticed that the difference between successive square numbers was always an odd number: $4-1=3$; $9-4=5$; $16-9=7$; $25-16=9$; and so on. Every once in a while that odd-number difference would itself be a square, as in $25-16=9$ (which is the same as $9+16=25$). When this happened, another right triangle could be built up from whole numbers.

For instance, Pythagoras might have subtracted the successive square numbers 144 and 169 as follows: $169-144=25$. It happens that the square roots of these numbers are 13, 12, and 5, since $169=13\times13$, $144=12\times12$, and $25=5\times5$. Therefore, he could form a right triangle with sides equal to five and twelve units and a hypotenuse equal to thirteen units.

Pythagorean Theorem

Pythagoras now had a large number of right triangles that were made up of hypotenuses whose squares were equal to the sum of the squares of the other two sides. And he soon proved that this situation was true for *all* right triangles.

Many hundreds of years before Pythagoras' time the Egyptians, the Babylonians, and the Chinese had known that such a relationship applied to the 3, 4, 5 triangle. In fact, the Babylonians and others probably had been sure that it applied to all right triangles. But Pythagoras was the first we know of who proved it.

He stated: *In any right triangle the sum of the squares of the sides is equal to the square of the hypotenuse.* Because he was the first to succeed in proving this statement, it is known as the "Pythagorean theorem." But how did he prove it?

Proof of Deduction

To answer that question, we must go back to the Greek thinker Thales, who was discussed in Chapter 1. Tradition holds that Pythagoras studied under Thales.

Thales had worked out an orderly system of proving the truth of mathematical statements, or *theorems*, by reasoning. One began with accepted statements called "axioms." From these axioms, one could reach a certain conclusion. With this conclusion accepted, a second conclusion could be obtained, and so on. Pythagoras used Thales' system, known as "deduction," to prove the Pythagorean theorem. And deduction has been used ever since.

Perhaps Thales did not actually invent the system of proof by deduction. Perhaps he learned it from the Babylonians and the name of the true inventor is unknown. But even if Thales was the inventor of mathematical deduction, it was Pythagoras who made it famous.

Birth of Geometry

The Greeks were inspired by the teachings of Pythagoras, especially by his great success in finding a deductive
proof for the Pythagorean theorem. As a result they went
even further. In the next three hundred years, they built
a complex structure of mathematical proofs that deal pri-
marily with lines and shapes. This system is called "geometry" (see Chapter 3).

We have gone far past the Greeks in the thousands of
years since. Yet, whatever we moderns have done in mathematics and however far we have penetrated its mysteries,
all rests on two foundations. There is, first, the study of
the properties of numbers and, second, the use of the
method of deduction. The first began with Pythagoras,
and the second was popularized by him.

It was not simply musical notes that Pythagoras had
plucked out of his cords, but the whole vast world of
mathematics.

3

Archimedes
and Applied Mathematics

You might think that an aristocrat in one of the greatest and richest of the Greek cities would have something better to do with his time than to study the workings of crowbars. Apparently the aristocrat thought so too, for he was embarrassed to have such a "low-bred" interest.

The aristocrat was Archimedes (ahr-kih-MEE-deez) of Syracuse, a city on the eastern shore of Sicily. Archimedes was born about 287 B.C. He was the son of a distinguished astronomer and was probably a relative of Hiero II, king of Syracuse.

An Inventor of Gadgets

In Archimedes' day it was felt that no gentleman should involve himself with engineering devices. Such matters were fit only for slaves and laborers. But Archimedes couldn't help it. Machinery interested him, and during his life he worked out many gadgets for use in both peace and war.

He didn't give in entirely to these "low" tastes, however. For instance, he didn't write up descriptions of his mechanical devices — he was ashamed to. We know of them only through the inaccurate and perhaps exaggerated tales of other men. The one exception is Archimedes' description of a device that imitated the heavenly motions of the sun, moon, and planets. But then, that was an instrument devoted to the science of astronmy and not to base mechanical labor.

Engineering — or Math?

Machines were not Archimedes' only interest. In his youth he had gone to Alexandria, in Egypt, the home of

the great Museum. The Museum was like a large university where all the learned Greeks came to study and teach.
There Archimedes had studied under Conon (KOH-non)
of Samos, a great mathematician. Archimedes himself became an even greater mathematician; he invented a form
of calculus two thousand years before modern mathematicians finally worked out all the details.

Thus, Archimedes had an interest in mathematics as
well as in engineering. However, in his time the two
fields had little in common.

It is true that the Greek and earlier engineers, such as
the Babylonians and Egyptians, had to use mathematics to
achieve what they did. The ancient Egyptians had built
great pyramids which were already ancient in Archimedes'
time. With only the most primitive tools the Egyptians
dragged immense blocks of granite many miles, then managed to raise them to great heights.

The people of Babylon also had built imposing structures, and the Greeks themselves had done well. A Greek
engineer named Eupalinus (yoo-puh-LIGH-nus) built a
tunnel on the island of Samos three centuries before Archimedes' time. He directed two teams of diggers at opposite
sides of a hill, and when they reached the hill's center, the
walls of the tunnel met almost exactly.

To do all this, the engineers of Egypt, Babylonia, and
Greece must have used mathematics. They must have
understood how lines were related to each other, and

how the size of one part of a structure determined the size of another.

Yet Archimedes was not familiar with this mathematics, but with an abstract kind the Greeks had begun to develop in Eupalinus' time.

Pythagoras had popularized the system of mathematical deduction (see Chapter 2). In this system one began with a few simple notions, readily accepted by all men, and reached complicated conclusions by proceeding one step at a time according to the principles of deduction.

Beautiful Theorem

Other Greek mathematicians followed Pythagoras and gradually built up a large and beautiful system of theorems (mathematical statements) about angles, parallel lines, triangles, squares, circles, and other figures. They learned how to show that two figures were equal in area or in angle size — or in both area and angle size. They found out how to determine ratios of numbers, size, and area.

Although the marvelous structure of Greek mathematics went far beyond the mathematics system of earlier civilizations, it was entirely theoretical. The circles and triangles were imaginary ones built of lines that were infinitely thin and perfectly straight or that were curved with perfect smoothness. The mathematics was not put to practical use.

Consider this story about the Greek philosopher Plato (PLAY-toe). He founded a school in Athens a century before Archimedes was born and taught mathematics at the school. One day during a mathematical demonstration a student asked Plato, "But master, of what practical use is this?" Plato was outraged. He ordered a slave to give the student a small coin so that he would find his learning had some use after all, and then expelled him from the school.

An important figure in the development of the Greek mathematics was the great mathematician Euclid (YOO-klid). One of Euclid's pupils was Conon of Samos, Archimedes' teacher. At Alexandria, shortly before Archimedes' birth, Euclid brought together all the deductions made by earlier thinkers. He organized them in beautiful order, demonstration by demonstration. And he began with a small handful of generally accepted statements, called "axioms." Axioms were so obvious, in the Greek view, that they required no proof. Examples of axioms are "a straight line is the shortest distance between two points" and "the whole is equal to the sum of its parts."

All Theory, No Practice

Euclid's book was so neatly done that it has been a text-book ever since. Still, in all its marvelous structure there was no hint that any of the conclusions might come in handy in the ordinary work of mankind. Indeed, the Greeks put their mathematics most thoroughly to use in working out the movements of the planets and in the theory of harmony. After all, astronomy and music were fit occupations for aristocrats.

So Archimedes excelled in two worlds — a practical world of engineering without the clever mathematics of the Greeks and a world of Greek mathematics that was put to no practical use. His abilities provided a perfect opportunity to combine the two worlds. But how would he do it?

A Marvelous Device

Consider the crowbar! Here is a simple mechanical device, but a marvelous one! Without the crowbar a huge boulder can be lifted only by the straining muscles of many men. But place a crowbar under the boulder and rest it on a pivot (such as a smaller rock), and a single man can easily raise the boulder.

Crowbars and similar devices are types of levers. The word "lever" comes from a Latin word meaning "to raise." Anything relatively long and rigid, such as a stick, a board, or a rod, can be used as a lever. A lever is such a simple device that even prehistoric men used it. But they didn't know how it worked, and neither did the clever Greek philosophers. The great Aristotle (AR-is-TOT-l), who had been a pupil of Plato's, noted that as one side of the lever pushed down and the other pulled up, both ends traced out circles in the air. He decided that the lever had wonderful properties because the circle had a wonderful shape.

Archimedes had experimented with levers, and he knew that Aristotle's explanation was incorrect. In his experiments Archimedes had rested a long lever on a pivot so as to balance it. If he placed a weight on only one end of the lever, that end went down. He could balance the lever by placing weights on both sides of the pivot. If the weights were equal, he could balance the lever by placing them in certain positions. If the weights were unequal, the balance came in other positions.

Language of Math

Archimedes found that levers behaved with great regularity. Why not use mathematics to explain this regularity? According to the principles of mathematical deduction, he would have to begin with an axiom, that is, something to be accepted without argument.

The axiom he used was based on the chief result of his experiments with levers. It went: *Equal weights at equal distances from the pivot will balance the lever. If equal weights are at unequal distances from the pivot, the side with the weight at the greater distance will go down.*

Archimedes then went on to use mathematical deduction to reach conclusions based on this axiom. These conclusions showed that the most important factors in the workings of any lever are the size of the weights or forces pressing down on it and their distances from the pivot.

Suppose a lever is balanced by unequal weights on opposite sides of the pivot. According to Archimedes' findings those unequal weights will have to be at different distances from the pivot. The distance of the small weight will be greater in order to make up for its smaller force. For example, a ten-pound weight twenty feet from the pivot will balance a one hundred-pound weight two feet from the pivot. The ten-pound weight is ten times lighter, so its distance is ten times greater.

This explains how one man can lift a huge boulder with a lever. When he places the pivot very near the boulder, his small force at a great distance from the pivot will balance the boulder's great weight at a small distance from the pivot.

Archimedes saw that if a man's force were applied at an extremely great distance from the pivot, an extremely huge weight could be lifted. "Give me a place to stand on," he is reported to have said, "and I can move the world."

But his work on the lever had already moved the world.

Archimedes was the first to apply Greek mathematics to practical engineering. In one stroke he had pioneered applied mathematics and founded the science of mechanics. He thus lit the fuse of a scientific revolution that was to explode eighteen centuries later.

4

Galileo and Experimentation

A YOUNG MAN of seventeen was attending services at the Cathedral of Pisa one Sunday in the year 1581. He was devoutly religious and no doubt tried to concentrate on his prayers. But he was distracted by a chandelier that hung nearby. An air current had caught the chandelier and set it swinging.

As it moved with the current, swinging gently at times

and through a wider arc at others, the young man noticed something. The chandelier seemed to keep steady time whether it swung through a wide arc or a narrow one. Wasn't that strange! Shouldn't it take longer to pass through a wide arc?

At this point the young man, whose name was Galileo (gal-ih-LEE-oh), must have forgotten the service completely. His eyes fastened on the swinging chandelier and the fingers of his right hand stole to his left wrist. While the organ music swelled about him, he counted his pulse beats. So many for one swing, so many for the next, and so on. The number of pulse beats was always the same, whether the swing was narrow or wide. In other words, the chandelier took just as long to swing through a narrow arc as through a wide one.

Galileo could hardly wait for the service to end. When it did, he rushed home and hung weights from strings. Timing their swings, he found that a weight suspended from a long string took a longer time to move back and forth than a weight suspended from a short string. However, when he studied each weight singly, he found it always took the same time to complete one swing, whether the swing was narrow or wide. Galileo had discovered the principle of the pendulum!

But he had done more than that. He had involved himself in a problem that had puzzled scholars for two thousand years — the problem of moving objects.

Ancient Theories

The ancients had observed that living things could move themselves and could also move nonliving objects. On the other hand, nonliving things usually could not move unless a living being moved them. But the ancients had observed many exceptions — the sea, the wind, the sun, the moon all moved without the help of living things. Another motion that did not depend on the living was the motion of falling bodies.

The Greek philosopher Aristotle felt that a falling motion was natural for all heavy things. It seemed to him that the heavier the falling object was, the more rapidly it fell. A pebble fell faster than a leaf, and a large pebble faster than a small one.

A century later Archimedes applied mathematics to physical situations, but only to motionless ones (see Chapter 3). He applied it to a lever in balance, for example. The problem of rapid motion was beyond even his great mind. For the next eighteen centuries no one challenged Aristotle's ideas of motion, and physics was at a standstill.

Slowing Falling Objects

By 1589 Galileo had finished his university training and was already famous for his work in mechanics. Like Archimedes he had applied mathematics to motionless situations. However, he longed to get back to the problem of motion.

If only there were some sure way, he thought, to slow down falling bodies so that he might experiment with them and study their motion in detail. (In an *experiment* a scientist sets up special conditions that will help him to study and observe phenomena more simply than he could in nature.)

Galileo remembered his pendulum. If a weight suspended from a string is pulled to one side and released, it starts falling. However, the string attached to it prevents it from falling straight down. Instead, the weight falls slantwise — and slowly enough so that it can be timed.

Unlike a freely falling body a pendulum weight does not fall in a straight line. This fact introduced complications. How could Galileo set up an experiment in which he could make a body move slantwise in a straight line?

Of course! Simply prepare a wooden board with a long, straight polished groove. Set balls rolling down that groove, and they will move in a straight line. And if the board is slanted nearly horizontal, the balls will roll quite slowly and one can study their motion in detail.

Galileo set balls of different weights rolling down the groove and timed them by counting the drops of water falling from a water-filled vessel with a small hole in the bottom. He found that except for very light objects, weight made no difference at all. All solid balls covered the length of the groove in the same time.

Aristotle Left Behind

All objects, Galileo decided, had to push the air out of the way as they fell. Very light objects could do so only with difficulty and were slowed by the resistance of the air. Heavier objects could do so easily and were not slowed. In a vacuum, where there was no air resistance at all, feathers and snowflakes would drop as quickly as pellets of lead.

Aristotle had stated that the speed of falling objects depended on their weight. Galileo proved that this was true only for exceptional cases, that is, for very light objects. And only because of air resistance. He was right, and Aristotle was wrong.

Next, Galileo marked off his long groove into small divisions of equal length. He found that any rolling ball covered each successive division in less time than it took to cover the one before. It was clear than an object accelerated as it fell. In other words it moved faster with each unit of time.

Galileo was able to work out simple mathematical relationships which he used to calculate the acceleration of a falling body. Thus, he applied mathematics to moving bodies as Archimedes had once applied it to motionless ones.

With this application and with the knowledge he had gained in his experiments with rolling balls, Galileo achieved astonishing results. For instance, he worked out exactly how a cannonball would move after it left the cannon.

Galileo was not the first to experiment, but his dramatic results with the problem of falling bodies made experimentation more popular in the world of science. No longer were scientists content merely to reason from axioms. Instead, they began to design experiments and make measurements. They could use experiments to check their reasoning and to serve as starting points for new reasoning. From 1589, then, we date the beginnings of *experimental science*.

For experimental science to succeed, however, accurate measurements of change had to be possible. Most of all, the passage of time itself had to be measured accurately.

Even in very ancient times mankind had learned to measure large units of time by means of astronomical changes. The steady march of the seasons marked off the year, the steady shift of the moon's phases marked off the month, the steady rotation of the earth marked off the day.

For units of time smaller than the day, mankind had to turn to less accurate methods. During the Middle Ages the mechanical clock had come into use. Hands were moved around a dial by geared wheels which were controlled by suspended weights. As the weights slowly fell, they turned the wheels.

But it was hard to regulate the fall of the weights and make the wheels turn smoothly and evenly. Therefore, such clocks always ran so fast or slow that none could be trusted to give the time closer than to the nearest hour.

Timekeeping Revolutionized

What was needed was some very steady motion that would regulate the turning wheels. In 1656 (fourteen years after Galileo's death) the Dutch scientist Christian Huygens (HIGH-genz) thought of the pendulum.

The pendulum beat out its swing in regular intervals. Suppose, then, that a pendulum was attached to a clock so that it controlled the gears. The movement of the gears would then become as regular as the swing of the pendulum.

Huygens managed to invent such a pendulum clock, or grandfather's clock, as it is often called. Based on a principle discovered by the young Galileo, Huygens' clock was mankind's first accurate timepiece and a boon to experimental science.

5

Democritus and Atoms

THEY CALLED him the "Laughing Philosopher" because he always seemed to be laughing bitterly at the foolishness of mankind.

His name was Democritus (dee-MOK-rih-tus) and he was born about 470 B.C. in the Greek city of Abdera. His fellow citizens may have thought his laughter the result of madness — one tradition says they considered him a lunatic and called in doctors to try to cure him.

To be sure, Democritus did seem to have peculiar notions. For instance, he worried about how far a drop of water could be divided. You could produce smaller and smaller drops of water until they were too small to see, but was there a limit? Did you eventually get a drop of water so small that it could be divided no more?

An End to Splitting?

Democritus' teacher, Leucippus (lyoo-SIP-us), had suspected there was a limit to division. Democritus continued thinking along these lines and finally announced his conviction that all substances could be divided only so far and no further. The smallest bit, or particle, of any kind of substance was indivisible. He called that smallest particle *atomos*, a Greek word meaning "indivisible." Democritus said the universe was made up of such tiny invisible particles. There was nothing in the universe but particles and the empty space between them.

According to Democritus, there were different types of these particles. They combined in various arrangements, and each arrangement formed a specific substance. If the substance iron rusted — that is, became the substance rust — it was because different kinds of particles in iron rearranged themselves. If ore turned to copper, the same. If wood burned and turned to ash, again the same.

Most Greek philosophers laughed at Democritus. How could anything be indivisible? A particle either did or didn't take up space. If it took up space, then it had to be capable of being broken in two, with each new particle taking up less space than the original. If the particle took up no space, then it was indivisible. But a particle taking up no space was nothing, and how could substances be built from nothing?

Either way, the philosophers decided, the notion of *atomos* was nonsense. No wonder people looked at Democritus suspiciously and wondered if he was sane. They didn't even think it worthwhile to make many copies of his books. Democritus wrote more than seventy books, but not one has survived.

To be sure, some philosophers did pick up the idea of indivisible particles. In 306 B.C., nearly a century after Democritus died, a philosopher named Epicurus (EP-ih-KYOO-rus) founded a school in Athens. He was a popular teacher and had many pupils. His style of philosophy was called Epicureanism, and it remained important for centuries. Part of this philosophy consisted of the particle theories of Democritus.

Nevertheless, even Epicurus couldn't convince his contemporaries, and his followers found themselves in a minority. Like the works of Democritus, none of the many books written by Epicurus has survived.

About 60 B.C. something fortunate happened. A Roman

poet named Lucretius (loo-CREE-shus) became interested in the Epicurean philosophy. He wrote a long poem, *On the Nature of Things*, in which he described the universe as composed of Democritus' indivisible particles. The book proved very popular and enough copies were made so that it survived ancient and medieval times. Through this one book the world learned in detail of Democritus' views.

In ancient times, books were hand-copied and expensive. As a result, only a few volumes of even the greatest works could be made and only the wealthy could afford to buy them. A great change occurred about 1450 A.D. with the invention of the printing press, which could turn out less expensive books by the thousands. One of the first works to be printed was Lucretius' *On the Nature of Things*.

Gassendi to Boyle

Thus, even the poorest scholars of early modern times could read the views of Democritus. Some of the scientists who did so were greatly impressed. A seventeenth-century French philosopher, Pierre Gassendi (ga-san-DEE), became a confirmed Epicurean. He argued strongly in favor of the theory of tiny indivisible particles.

One of Gassendi's pupils was an Englishman named Robert Boyle. In 1660 Boyle was studying air and wondered why it could be compressed, or made to take up less and less space.

He supposed that air was made up of tiny particles with a great deal of space between them. Compressing the air would mean pushing the particles more closely together. There would be less empty space between particles. That made sense.

On the other hand, water might be made up of particles that were close together, so close that they were in contact. For that reason, it seemed to Boyle, liquid water could not be compressed any further. However, if the particles were pulled far apart, the water would become water vapor, a thin air-like substance.

So Boyle also became a follower of Democritus.

Thus, for two thousand years there was an unbroken chain of believers in a theory of indivisible particles: Democritus, Epicurus, Lucretius, Gassendi, and Boyle. Nevertheless, their views were never accepted by the majority. "What! A particle that can't be broken into smaller particles? Nonsense!"

Weight Watchers

However, in the eighteenth century, chemists began to reconsider the way in which chemical compounds were formed. They knew that other substances combined to form these compounds. For example, copper, oxygen, and carbon combined to form the compound copper carbonate. For the first time, however, they began to measure the relative weights of the combining substances.

Toward the end of the century a French chemist, Joseph Louis Proust (PROOST), went into such measurements in great detail. He found, for instance, that whenever copper, oxygen, and carbon formed copper carbonate, they always combined in the same proportion by weight. The proportion, or ratio, was five units of copper to four units of oxygen to one unit of carbon. In other words, if Proust used up five ounces of copper to form the compound, he would also have to use up four ounces of oxygen and one ounce of carbon.

It wasn't as though he were baking a cake, where he could increase the flour a bit, if he chose, or cut down on the milk. There was no way to change the "recipe" for copper carbonate. Whatever Proust did, the proportion was always 5 to 4 to 1 and never anything else.

He tried other substances and he found the same effect — always one recipe. By 1799 he announced his results. Out of these results came what we now know as "Proust's law" or "the law of definite proportions."

"Odd!" thought the English chemist John Dalton when Proust announced his results. "Why should this be?"

Dalton thought of the possibility of indivisible particles. What if an oxygen particle always weighed four times as

much as a carbon particle and a copper particle always
weighed five times as much as a carbon particle? Then, if
you made copper carbonate by combining a copper particle, an oxygen particle, and a carbon particle, you would
have the ratio 5 to 4 to 1.

If you wanted to alter the ratio of copper carbonate
slightly, you would have to chip a piece off one of the
three particles. Since Proust and other chemists were
showing that the ratio of a compound couldn't be changed,
it meant the particles couldn't be chipped. Dalton decided
they were indivisible, just as Democritus had thought.

Dalton searched for more evidence. He found different
compounds that were made up of the same substances.
However, the proportion of the substances in each compound was different. For example, carbon dioxide was
composed of carbon and oxygen in the ratio by weight of
three units of carbon to eight units of oxygen. Carbon
monoxide was also made up of carbon and oxygen, but in
the ratio of 3 to 4.

This was interesting. The number of carbon weight
units was the same in both ratios — three units in carbon
monoxide and three units in carbon dioxide. So there
might be one carbon particle weighing three units in each
compound.

At the same time, the eight units of oxygen in the carbon
dioxide ratio exactly doubled the four units in the carbon
monoxide ratio. If an oxygen particle weighed four units,

Dalton thought, then perhaps carbon monoxide was partly composed of one oxygen particle and carbon dioxide of two.

Then Dalton may have remembered the copper carbonate. The weight ratio of carbon to oxygen had been 1 to 4 (which is the same ratio as 3 to 12). This ratio could be explained if you assumed that copper carbonate was made up of one carbon and three oxygen particles. Always you could work out a system whereby whole numbers of particles were involved, never fractions.

By 1803 Dalton had announced his theory of indivisible particles. This time, however, the statement differed from those previously proclaimed. No longer was the theory merely a belief. Dalton had a whole century's worth of chemical experimentation to back him up.

Atoms by Experiment

The change in science brought about by Galileo proved its worth (see Chapter 4). Argument alone had never convinced mankind of the existence of indivisible particles, but argument plus experimental results did so almost at once.

Dalton recognized that his view dated back to the Laughing Philosopher, and he humbly made use of Democritus' word *atomos* to show this recognition. In English the word became "atom." Dalton had established the atomic theory.

All of chemistry was revolutionized as a result. In 1900, physicists used methods no one had previously dreamed of to discover that the atom was made up of still smaller particles, and the science of physics was revolutionized. Then, when energy was drawn from within the atom to produce atomic power, the course of human history began to be revolutionized.

6

Lavoisier and Gases

It's hard to believe that air is really something. You can't see it and normally you don't feel it, and yet it's there. If it moves quickly enough, it becomes a storm blast that can wreck ships and blow down trees. Its presence can't be denied.

Is air the only substance that can't be seen? The alchemists of the Middle Ages seemed to think so. When their concoctions gave off colorless bubbles or vapors, they recorded that they had formed "an air."

If alchemists existed today, we would not take many of their findings seriously. After all, alchemy was a false science that was more interested in converting other metals to gold than in adding to our knowledge of matter. However, some able alchemists observed and studied the behavior of the metals and other substances they worked with. In this way, they made important discoveries that contributed to modern chemistry.

An Able Alchemist

One of these talented alchemists was Jan Baptista van Helmont. Actually, he was a physician and only dabbled in alchemy. About 1630, van Helmont felt dissatisfied with the notion that all colorless vapors were really air. The "airs" he found bubbling out of his mixtures just didn't seem to be air at all.

For instance, when he placed bits of silver into a strong chemical called nitric acid, the silver dissolved and a red vapor bubbled up and curled into the space above the surface of the liquid. Was this air? Who had ever heard of red air? Who had ever heard of air that could be seen?

Then, when van Helmont added limestone to vinegar,

bubbles rose to the top of the liquid again. These at least were colorless and looked just like air bubbles. But if he held a lighted candle above the liquid's surface, the flame went out. What kind of air was it in which a candle would not burn? The same flame-quenching vapors rose from fermenting fruit juice and from smoldering wood.

So, the so-called airs that van Helmont and other alchemists produced were not really air. But they were so much like air that they fooled everyone — that is, everyone but van Helmont. He decided that air was just one example of a group of airlike substances.

These substances were harder to study than ordinary materials, which could easily be seen and felt. Ordinary substances had definite shapes and took up definite amounts of room. They came in pieces and quantities — a lump of sugar, half a glass of water. The airlike substances did not. They seemed to spread out thinly everywhere and to have no structure.

From "Chaos" to "Gas"

A new group of substances needed a name. Van Helmont knew the Greek myth that the universe began with thin matter without structure that spread out everywhere. The Greeks called that original matter *chaos*. There was a good word! But van Helmont was Flemish — that is, he lived in what is now Belgium — and he pronounced the old Greek word in good Flemish fashion. He spelled it as he pronounced it, and the word became "gas."

Van Helmont was the first to realize that air was but one kind of gas and that there also were other kinds of gas. Nowadays, we call his red gas nitrogen dioxide and his flame-quenching gas carbon dioxide.

Van Helmont found it difficult to study the gases because as soon as they formed, they mixed with air and faded away. However, about one hundred years later an English minister, Stephen Hales, thought of a way to prevent that diffusion.

Hales let the gas bubbles form in a vessel whose only opening was a bent pipe. The pipe led under water, into the mouth of an upside-down water-filled bottle. The bubbles traveled through the pipe and up into the bottle, forcing out the water, giving Hales a bottle full of some particular gas, with which he could then experiment.

Priestley's New Drink

Unfortunately, some gases could not be collected in a water-filled bottle because they dissolve in water. However, about 1770, another English minister, Joseph Priestley, substituted mercury for water. Gases did not dissolve in mercury, so it could be used to collect any gas.

Priestley collected van Helmont's two gases by using mercury. He was particularly interested in carbon dioxide. Once he had collected the gas over mercury, he dissolved some in water and found that a pleasant drink resulted. He had invented soda water.

Priestley also collected the gases ammonia, hydrogen chloride, and sulfur dioxide and he discovered oxygen. Obviously, there were dozens of different gases.

A Burning Issue

About the same time that Priestley was discovering gases, in the 1770's, the French chemist Antoine-Laurent Lavoisier (lah-vwah-ZYAY) was wrapped up in the problem of combustion. Combustion — that is, the burning or rusting of substances in air — was a process that nobody really understood.

Of course, Lavoisier wasn't the first to study combustion. But he had an advantage over his predecessors: He firmly believed that accurate measurements were important in an experiment. The idea of making careful measurements was not new. It had been introduced two hundred years before by Galileo (see Chapter 4). However, it was Lavoisier who extended the idea to chemistry.

Therefore, Lavoisier didn't just watch substances burning and examine the ash that was left behind. And he didn't just watch metals rusting and examine the rust, that is, the dull or crumbly substance that formed on their surface. Before a substance burned or rusted, he carefully measured its weight. And after combustion he weighed it again.

At first these measurements brought only confusion. Wood burned and the ash it left behind was much *lighter* than the original wood. A candle burned and was gone altogether; nothing at all was left behind. Lavoisier and some friends bought a small diamond and heated it until it also burned. That vanished, too. Did burning a material destroy part or all of its substance?

On the other hand, Lavoisier found that when metals rusted, the rust was *heavier* than the original metal. Additional solid material seemed to come from nowhere. Why should rusting add matter, while burning seemed to destroy it?

A Weighty Problem

Earlier chemists had not worried very much about such things because they weren't acustomed to weighing their chemicals. Lighter? Heavier? What difference did it make?

But Lavoisier worried about it. Did burned material vanish into thin air? Ah, perhaps that was it. If substances formed gases when they burned, wouldn't those gases do just that? Wouldn't they mix with the air and vanish into it?

Van Helmont had shown that burning wood produced carbon dioxide. Lavoisier had obtained the same gas from his burning diamond. Thus, it was certain that combustion could produce gas. But *how much* gas was formed? Was it enough to make up for the loss of weight?

Lavoisier thought that might be the case. About twenty years earlier a Scottish chemist, Joseph Black, had heated limestone (calcium carbonate) and found that it released carbon dioxide. The limestone lost weight, but the weight of the gas produced equaled that lost weight.

"Well then," Lavoisier thought, "suppose a burning substance loses weight because it releases a gas. Then what about metals? Did they gain weight when they rust because they combine with a gas?"

Black's work again provided a clue. He had bubbled carbon dioxide gas through limewater (a solution of calcium hydroxide), and the gas and calcium hydroxide combined to form powdered limestone. If calcium hydroxide could combine with a gas to form another substance, Lavoisier thought, then perhaps metals did the same.

Locking Air Out

Thus, Lavoisier had good reason to suspect that gases were behind the weight changes that resulted from combustion. But how would he prove his suspicion? Weighing ashes and rusts was not enough; he also would have to weigh the gases.

However, the wide blanket of air that encircles the earth created a problem. How could he weigh gases that escaped from burning objects into the air? On the other hand, how could he determine the amount of gas that left the air to combine with a metal, when more air would rush in to take its place?

The answer, Lavoisier realized, was to lock in the gases and lock out all but a definite amount of air. He could do both by conducting his chemical reactions in a sealed container. Then, if a substance inside it burned and released gases, they would be captured in the container. If a substance rusted and combined with gases, they would come only from the air inside the container.

Weighing the Evidence

Lavoisier began by carefully weighing the container with the solid substance and air sealed inside it. He heated the enclosed substance by focusing sunlight on it with a large magnifying glass or by building a fire under it. When the substance had burned or rusted, he again weighed the container with its contents.

He repeated the process with a number of different substances. In every case, regardless of what it was that burned or rusted, the sealed container showed no change in weight.

Suppose, for example, a piece of wood burned to an ash, which of course weighed less than the wood. The weight of the gas released by the wood made up the missing weight. Therefore, the weight of the container remained the same.

Suppose a piece of iron absorbed gas from the air in the container and changed into rust. The rust was heavier than the iron. However, the weight gained was exactly offset by the air's loss of weight. Again, the weight of the container did not change.

Lavoisier's experiments and measurements had a great influence on the development of chemistry. They laid the groundwork for his interpretation of combustion, the interpretation we still use today. The experiments also led him to conclude that matter could be neither created nor destroyed; it could only change from one form to another (for example, from solid substance to gas).

This is the famous "law of conservation of matter." This idea that matter is indestructible made it easier to accept, thirty years later, the theory that matter is made up of indestructible atoms (see Chapter 5).

Both the law of conservation of matter and the atomic theory have been improved and slightly changed in the twentieth century. On the whole, however, they form the strong and sturdy platform on which modern chemistry stands. For his part in building this platform, Lavoisier is commonly called the "father of modern chemistry."

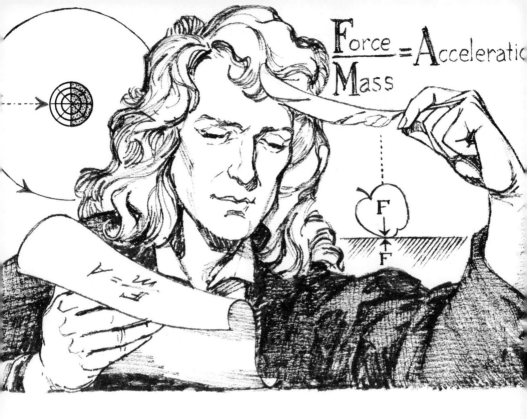

7

Newton and Inertia

It's only natural to think that the universe is made up of two parts — the heavens and the earth. And to the ancient Greek philosopher Aristotle the two parts seemed to operate in completely different ways.

Aristotle observed that everything on earth changed or decayed — men grew old and died, buildings aged and crumbled, the sea became stormy then calm, winds blew clouds here and there, fires blazed up and went out, the very land shivered with earthquakes.

In the sky, however, there seemed to be only serenity and changelessness. The sun rose and set on schedule, its flame never brighter or dimmer. The moon went through its phases in regular order, and the stars shone without ceasing.

Aristotle decided that the two parts of the universe operated under different sets of rules or "natural laws." There was one natural law for objects on earth and another for objects in the heavens.

These different natural laws also seemed to apply when Aristotle considered the way objects moved. For example, if a stone was held in the air and released, it dropped straight down. On a windless day, smoke rose straight up. Left to itself, all earthly motion seemed to be either up or down.

Not so in the sky. The sun and moon and stars didn't fall toward the earth or rise away from it. Instead, Aristotle thought they moved in smoth, steady circles around the earth.

One more difference. On earth, moving objects eventually stopped. A falling rock hit the earth and came to rest. A falling ball might bounce a few times, but soon it also came to rest. A sliding block of wood, a rolling wagon, a kicked pebble — all came to rest. Even a running horse eventually tired and stood still.

Thus, it seemed to Aristotle that the natural state of things on earth was rest. Anything in motion returned to that natural state of rest as soon as possible. In the sky, however, the sun, moon, and stars never stopped, but kept moving forever at the same stately speed.

Galileo to Newton

Aristotle's notions about the way objects move were the best the human mind had to offer for nearly two thousand years. Then Galileo began to come up with better ones (see Chapter 4).

Where Aristotle had thought that heavy objects fell more rapidly than light ones, Galileo showed that all objects fell at the same speed. However, Aristotle was right about very light objects. They fell more slowly, it was true. But Galileo explained why they were slowed down. They were so light, they could push through the air only with difficulty. In a vacuum, he said, even the lightest object would fall as quickly as a lump of lead because it would no longer be slowed by air resistance.

About forty years after Galileo's death the English scientist Isaac Newton examined the idea that a moving object could be affected by air resistance. He could think of other ways in which motion was interfered with.

For example, when a falling object hit the earth, its motion stopped because the ground got in its way. When a rock skidded across a dirt road, the ground still got in its way. The rock was stopped by friction between the uneven surface of the road and rough spots on its own surface.

When a rock moved along a smooth paved road, there was less friction and it moved farther before stopping. Along a stretch of ice it moved still farther.

What would happen, Newton thought, if a moving object made no contact with anything at all? What if there were no barriers, no friction, no air resistance? In other words, what if the object were moving through a vast vacuum?

In that case, there would be nothing to stop it, slow it, or swerve it from its path — nothing at all. The object would just keep moving at the same speed and in the same direction forever. Therefore, Newton decided that the natural state of an object on earth was not necessarily rest. That was only part of it.

He set forth his conclusions in a statement which can be expressed as follows: *Any object at rest left entirely to itself will remain at rest forever. Any object in motion left entirely to itself will move at the same speed in the same straight line forever.*

This statement is called Newton's first law of motion.

According to Newton, objects tended to stay at rest or in motion. They seemed almost too "idle" or "lazy" to change their state. For this reason, Newton's first law of motion is sometimes called the principle of "inertia." ("Inertia" comes from a Greek word meaning "idleness.")

If you think about it, you can see that different objects have different amounts of inertia, or resistance to change. Suppose you want to set a beach ball moving. You give it a light touch and off it sails. If you want to set a cannonball moving, however, you have to push it as hard as you can and even so, it moves but slowly.

Once the two are moving, there is a difference in the ease with which they can be stopped. You can stop a quickly moving beach ball by batting it down with your hand. A cannonball moving at the same speed had better not be interfered with, for it would knock your hand painfully to one side and scarcely be affected itself.

The cannonball is much more reluctant to change its state of motion than is a beach ball. The cannonball has much more inertia. Newton suggested that the *mass* of an object was the amount of the object's inertia. Thus, a cannonball has more mass than a beach ball.

A cannonball also has more weight than a beach ball. In general, heavy objects have considerable mass while light objects have little mass. However, weight is not the same as mass. On the moon, for instance, any object is only one-sixth as heavy as it is on earth, but its mass is unchanged. The movement of a canonball on the moon would be as

hard to start and as dangerous to stop as on earth. Yet, the
cannonball would seem surprisingly light if you were hold-
ing it.

To make an object move faster, slow down, or turn
aside on its path, you must push or pull it. A push or a pull
is called a "force." The rate at wich a body is made to
quicken or slow its motion or to turn aside is its "acceleration."

Newton also put forth a second law of motion, which
may be stated as follows: *The acceleration of any body is
equal to the force applied to that body divided by the
body's mass.* In other words, pushing or pulling an object
tends to speed it up, slow it down, or turn it aside. The
greater the force, the more the object will change its speed
or direction. On the other hand, the object's mass — that
is, the amount of inertia it has — acts against this acceleration. For example, a hard push will make a beach ball go
much faster because it has little mass. But the same force
applied to the much more massive cannonball will hardly
affect its movement.

From Apple to Moon

Newton then went on to propose a third law of motion,
which may be stated: *If a body exerts a force on a second
body, then that second body exerts an equal force, in the*

opposite direction, on the first body. In other words, if a book presses down on a table, the table must be pressing up on the book by just an equal amount. That is why the book stays in place, neither sinking through the table nor bounding into the air.

Those three laws of motion can be used to explain almost all the motions and forces on earth. Can they also explain the much different motions in the heavens?

The objects in the heavens move through a vacuum, but not in a straight line. The moon, for instance, follows a curved path around the earth. Does this fact contradict Newton's first law? No, because the moon is not being "left entirely to itself." It doesn't move in a straight line because it is always being pulled to one side — in the direction of the earth.

In order for the moon to be pulled to one side like that, Newton's second law required the existence of a force applied to the moon, a force always exerted in the direction of the earth.

The earth does, of course, exert a force on earthly bodies. It makes apples fall downward, for instance. This is the *force of gravitation.* Could this force also affect the moon? Newton applied his three laws of motion to the moon and showed that its movements could be explained nicely if one supposed that it is affected by the earth's force of gravitation in the same way as an apple.

What's more, a force of gravitation is set up by every

object in the universe. It is the gravitation of the sun, for instance, that keeps the earth moving around that large, glowing body.

Newton was able to use his three laws of motion to show that the size of the force of gravitation between any two bodies in the universe depended on the masses of the bodies and on the distance between them. The greater the masses, the greater the gravitational force. The greater the distance between the bodies, the smaller the gravitational force. Newton had worked out the law of *universal* gravitation.

Two great things were accomplished by this law. First, it explained the motions of the heavenly bodies down to almost the finest detail. It explained why our earth wobbled very slowly on its axis. Eventually it also was used to explain how pairs of stars many trillions of miles away from us circled each other.

Even more important, perhaps, Newton showed that Aristotle was wrong in concluding that there were two sets of natural laws, one for the heavens and one for the earth. The three laws of motion explained falling apples and bouncing balls, as well as the circling moon. Thus, Newton proved that the heavens and the earth were parts of the same universe.

8

Faraday and Fields

IMAGINE AN iron rod standing on its end, with a string tied about it near the top. Can you knock it over?

Certainly you can. Just push it with your finger or seize the string and pull it. The push or the pull is a *force*. In almost all cases a force is delivered only when the two objects touch.

When you push the rod, your finger touches it. When

you pull it, your fingers hold the string and the string touches the rod. You might knock the rod over without seeming to touch it, just by blowing in its direction. But then you push air molecules in the direction of the rod, and they touch it and push it.

Newton's three laws of motion explained the behavior of such forces (see Chapter 7). The laws could be used to explain the principles underlying machines in which levers, pulleys, and gears acted by pushing and pulling. In such machines, objects exerted forces on other objects by making contact.

"Mechanical" Universe

In the 1700's, scientists believed the whole universe ran by such contact forces. This was the *mechanical view* of the universe.

Could there be forces without contact? Indeed there could. One was the force of gravitation, which Newton himself had explained. The earth pulled at the moon and kept it in its orbit, but the earth did not touch the moon. There was absolutely nothing between the two bodies, not even air; yet there was a considerable force of gravitation between them.

We can observe another kind of force without contact if we return to our iron rod standing on end. All we need is a small magnet. Bring that magnet close to the top of the

rod and the rod will lean toward the magnet and fall. The
magnet doesn't have to touch the rod; nor is the air involved, for the magnet will pull at the rod in a vacuum.

If a thin, long magnet is allowed to swing in any direction, it will end up pointing north and south. In other
words, the magnet will become a simple compass. With
such compasses, European navigators began to explore the
oceans about 1350.

The end of the magnet that points north is called its
north pole; the other end is its south pole. If the north pole
of one magnet is brought near the south pole of another,
there is a strong pull between the magnets and they will
come together. If like poles — that is, north and north or
south and south — are brought near one another, there is
a strong push and the magnets will move apart.

This kind of force-without-touching is called "action at
a distance" and it puzzled scientists from the beginning.
Even Thales (see Chapter 1) was taken aback when he first
observed that lumps of a certain black ore attracted iron at
a distance. "This ore must have life in it!" he exclaimed.

It didn't, of course. It was only ordinary loadstone. But
how else were scientists going to explain the mysterious
force of a magnet, a force which could attract and topple
an iron rod without touching it? The action of a compass
was even more mysterious. Its magnetic needle always
pointed north and south because it was attracted by the
distant polar regions of the earth. Here was action at a

very great distance! Here was a force that could find a magnetic needle in a haystack!

In 1831 the English scientist Michael Faraday attacked the problem of these mysterious forces. He placed two magnets on a wooden table, with the north pole of one facing the south pole of the other. The magnets were close enough to pull at each other, but not close enough to come together. At this distance their force wasn't strong enough to overcome their friction with the table. Faraday knew the force was there, however, for if he dropped iron filings between the magnets, they moved up to the magnets and clung there.

Faraday decided to vary the experiment. He laid a piece of sturdy paper over the two magnets, then dropped the filings on the paper. The friction of the filings against the paper held them in place and kept them from moving toward the magnets.

Magnetic "Line-up"

Then Faraday tapped the paper lightly to make the filings move a bit. Promptly they twisted like tiny compass needles and pointed toward one magnet or the other.

Indeed, the filings seemed to take up a position in lines that extended from the pole of one magnet to the pole of the other. Faraday considered this carefully. The lines exactly between the two poles were straight. A little to one side of the space between the magnets the filings still lined up, but now they traced out a curve. The farther the filings were to one side, the farther outward was the curve they traced.

Faraday snapped his fingers. He had it! There were *magnetic lines of force* passing from the north pole of a magnet to its own south pole or to the south pole of another magnet. And these lines of force could move outward great distances from the poles.

This meant that the magnet didn't work by action at a distance at all. Instead, a magnet pushed or pulled at some object when its lines of force approached it. The magnet's lines of force either touched the object or approached lines of force that came from the object itself.

Later scientists came to suspect that the same thing probably happened in other kinds of action at a distance. There had to be *gravitational lines of force,* for instance, around the earth and moon. It was these touching lines of force that enable the two bodies to attract each other. Then, too, electrically charged bodies pushed and pulled at objects, so there were also *electrical lines of force.*

New Generators

Faraday was quickly able to show that when objects moved across magnetic lines of force, an electric current was set up in the moving object.

Until then, electric currents could be obtained only from batteries, which are containers of reacting chemicals. Battery electricity was quite expensive. With Faraday's new discovery, electricity could be generated by a steam engine, which could move objects across magnetic lines of force. Electricity obtained from such steam *generators* was very cheap and could be produced in enormous quantities. Thus, it was magnetic lines of force that electrified the world in the twentieth century.

Faraday was a self-taught genius. He had not been to school past the earliest grades, and he knew no mathematics. He could not work out a mathematical description of how the lines of force were distributed about a magnet. He could only trace them with his iron filings.

About 1860, however, a Scottish mathematician by the name of James Clerk Maxwell tackled the problem. Maxwell worked out a set of mathematical equations which described how the strength of force changed as one went farther and farther away from a magnet in any direction.

The force surrounding a magnet is called a "field." The field of any magnet fills the entire universe. However, it rapidly grows weak as distance increases, so it can be measured only quite close to the magnet. Maxwell showed that a line could be drawn through all parts of the field that had a particular strength. The result would be one of the lines of force that Faraday spoke of. Maxwell's equations thus made it possible to deal exactly with Faraday's lines of force.

Maxwell also showed that magnetic fields and electric fields always existed together. Thus, one could speak only of an *electromagnetic field*. Under certain conditions a set of "waves" spread out in all directions from the center of such a field. This was *electromagnetic radiation*. Such radiation had to travel at the speed of light, according to Maxwell's mathematics. Thus, it seemed that light itself was an electromagnetic radiation.

Years after Maxwell died, his theories were proved correct. New kinds of electromagnetic radiation, such as radio waves and X rays, were discovered. Maxwell had predicted these kinds of radiation, but he did not live to see their existence proved by experiment.

In 1905 the German-Swiss scientist Albert Einstein began to revamp man's view of the universe. He abandoned the mechanical view, which had begun with Newton's laws of motion, and explained the universe in terms of fields.

The two fields that were known at the time were the gravitational field and the electromagnetic field. Einstein tried to find a single set of mathematical equations that would describe both fields, but failed. Since his time, however, two new fields have been discovered which apply to the tiny particles that make up the nucleus, or core, of the atom. These are known as "nuclear fields."

Electromagnet Push-Pull

Everything that used to be considered a push-pull force is now viewed as the interaction of fields. The rims of atoms consist of electrons. When two atoms approach each other, the electromagnetic fields surrounding these electrons push one another. The atoms themselves move apart without having actually touched.

Therefore, when we push a rod or pull a string, we are not really making contact with anything solid. We are just taking advantage of these tiny electromagnetic fields. The moon circles the earth and the earth circles the sun because of the gravitational fields about these bodies. Atomic bombs explode because of things that happen to nuclear fields.

The new *field view* of the universe has helped scientists make advances that would have been impossible in the days of the mechanical view. Yet, the field view traces right back to Faraday's idea that magnetic lines of force could push or pull an object.

9

Rumford and Heat

It is difficult to have much sympathy for Benjamin Thompson. He was a shrewd person whose first and last concern was for himself. When he was only nineteen, for instance, he escaped the poverty of his childhood by marrying a rich widow nearly twice his age.

Thompson was born in Woburn, Massachusetts, in

1753. In those days, Massachusetts and the other original American states were still British colonies. A few years after Thompson was married, the American Revolution broke out and he guessed wrong as to which side would win. He attached himself to the British army in Boston and served as a spy against the colonial patriots.

When the British left Boston, they took Thompson with them. He left his wife and child behind with no apparent misgivings and never returned.

In Europe, he served any government that would pay his price — and got in trouble with one after another because he took bribes, sold secrets, and in general was an immoral and dishonest man.

In 1790, Thompson left England for the European continent. He entered the service of Bavaria (now part of Germany, but then an independent nation), and the Bavarian ruler granted him the title of count. Thompson called himself Count Rumford, "Rumford" being the original name of Concord, New Hampshire, where he had married his first wife. It is as Rumford that Benjamin Thompson is now known in history.

Scientific Mind

There is one thing to be said in Rumford's favor: He had a strong yearning for knowledge. From boyhood, he showed an active and shrewd mind that could pierce to the core of a problem.

In the course of his life, Rumford conducted many interesting experiments and came to many important conclusions. But the most important of all took place in Bavaria, after he had been placed in charge of manufacturing cannons. A cannon was made by casting metal in the proper shape. The solid metal then was hollowed out to form the interior of the cannon. A rapidly turning boring tool was used to scrape and gouge out the interior.

Of course, the cannon and the boring tool grew hot. Streams of cold water had to be sprayed on them constantly. Rumford watched the heat develop and his active mind began to work.

Just what was heat anyway?

Scientists of the time, including the great French chemist Lavoisier, felt that heat was a weightless fluid they called *caloric*. As more caloric was squeezed into a substance, that substance grew hotter and hotter. Eventually, the caloric overflowed and streamed out in all directions. Thus, you could feel the warmth from a red-hot object at quite a distance. The warmth of the sun, for example, could be felt at a distance of 93,000,000 miles. If a hot object was placed in contact with a cold one, caloric flowed out of the hot object and into the cold. The flow caused the hot object to cool down and the cold object to warm up.

The theory worked quite well and very few scientists questioned it. But Rumford did. He wondered why the caloric was pouring out of the cannon. People who believed in the caloric theory said it was because the boring tool was breaking the metal inside the cannon to bits. The caloric contained in the metal therefore came pouring out like water from a broken jug.

Indeed? Rumford looked over the boring tools and found one that was completely blunted and worn down. "Use that one," he said. The workers objected that it was used up, but Rumford repeated his order more sharply and they scurried to their labors.

The blunt borer turned uselessly. It did not cut through the metal at all, but it developed even more heat than a new borer. The workers must have wondered why the count looked so pleased.

Rumford saw that caloric was *not* released through the break-up of the metal. In fact, did it come from the metal at all? The metal was cold to begin with, so it couldn't have held much caloric. Yet caloric seemed to flow out in unlimited quantities.

Rumford measured the caloric flowing out of the cannon by noting how much the water was heated up as it cooled the boring tool and cannon. If all that caloric were put back into the cannon, he concluded, the cannon would melt.

Particles in Motion

Rumford decided that heat was not a fluid at all, but a form of motion. As the borer ground against the metal, its motion was converted into quick, tiny motions of the particles making up the metal. It didn't matter whether the borer cut or did not cut through the metal. It was those quick, tiny particle-motions that resulted in heat. Naturally, heat would continue to be produced as long as the boring tool turned. Heat production had nothing to do with any caloric that might or might not be in the metal.

For fifty years afterward, Rumford's work was ignored. Scientists were content to deal with caloric, and to work out theories explaining how it flowed from one body to another.

Why? Part of the reason was that they hesitated to accept the idea of tiny particles undergoing a quick, tiny motion that no one could see.

About ten years after Rumford's work, however, John Dalton advanced the atom theory (see Chapter 5). Little by little, scientists were accepting the existence of atoms. Wasn't it possible, then, that Rumford's small moving particles were atoms or molecules (groups of atoms)?

Perhaps. But how was one to imagine the motion of trillions upon trillions of invisible molecules? Did they all

move together? Did some move one way and some another, according to some neat pattern? Or did they undergo *random motion,* each one moving in any direction
and at any speed, with no way of telling the direction and
speed of any particular molecule?

If the molecules did engage in random movement, how
could one possibly make sense out of such a condition?

In the middle 1700's, a few decades before Rumford's
work, a Swiss mathematician named Daniel Bernoulli had
tried to handle the problem of random motion of particles
in gases. This attempt was well before scientists accepted
an atomic theory, and Bernoulli's mathematics wasn't quite
detailed enough. Still, it was a good try.

In the 1860's, James Clerk Maxwell came on the scene
(see Chapter 8). Maxwell assumed that the molecules
making up gases were engaged in random movement. By
keen mathematical analysis, he showed how random move-
movement provided a neat explanation of the behavior of
gases.

Maxwell showed how particles of gas moving at random
could create a pressure against the walls of a vessel that
held them. Furthermore, that pressure would change if
the particles were forced together or if they were allowed
to spread apart. This explanation of the behavior of gases
is known as the kinetic theory of gases. ("Kinetic" comes
from a Greek word meaning "motion.")

Maxwell usually shares the credit for the theory with

the Austrian physicist Ludwig Boltzmann. The two men worked it out independently at about the same time.

Maxwell's Solution

One of the important laws of gas behavior states that a gas expands as temperature goes up and contracts as temperature goes down. According to the caloric theory, the explanation for this behavior was simple. As a gas heats up, caloric pours into it. More caloric needs more room, so the gas expands. As a gas cools, caloric leaves and the gas contracts.

What did Maxwell have to say to that? Rumford's experiment must have been in his mind. Heat is a form of motion. As a gas is heated, its molecules move faster and faster and nudge each other farther apart. Thus the gas expands. When the temperature drops, the reverse happens and the gas contracts.

Maxwell worked out an equation which showed the range of speed that gas molecules would have at any given temperature. Some molecules moved slowly and some quickly, but most moved at an intermediate speed. Among these various speeds, one particular speed was most probable at a given temperature. As the temperature rose, this most probable speed increased.

This *kinetic theory of heat* could apply to liquids and

solids, as well as gases. In a solid, for instance, molecules might not fly about like bullets, as they did in gases. Instead, they might vibrate about one spot. The speed of this variation followed Maxwell's equation, as did the speed of the bulletlike molecules in gases.

A Better Explanation

All the properties of heat could be explained just as well by the kinetic theory as by the caloric theory. Indeed, the kinetic theory easily accounted for some properties (such as those described by Rumford) which the caloric theory had failed to explain adequately.

The caloric theory had described heat transfer as the flow of caloric from a hot object into a cold one. According to the kinetic theory, heat transfer resulted from the movement of molecules. When a hot body was placed in contact with a cold one, its fast-moving molecules collided with the slow ones of the cold body. As a result, the fast molecules slowed down a bit and the slow ones speeded up. Thus, heat "flowed" from the hot body to the cold.

The understanding of heat as a form of motion is one of the great ideas of science. Maxwell enlarged this great idea into an even greater one. He showed how random motion could be used to explain certain definite laws of nature whose effect was totally predictable, not random at all.

Maxwell's idea has been expanded very much in the past century. Scientists now take it for granted that the random behavior of atoms and molecules can bring about the most amazing results. Even life itself may have been created from the nonliving matter in the oceans through the random movements of atoms and molecules.

10

Joule and Energy

From prehistoric times, man has realized that motion can accomplish tasks and do work. Place a rock on a nut and nothing will happen. But set the rock in motion by quickly bringing it down on the nut, and the nut will crack. Similarly, an arrow in rapid flight can force its way through the thick hide of an animal. And many of us have seen wreckers shatter a brick wall by swinging a ponderous steel ball against it.

The ability to do work is called "energy." A moving object possesses energy of motion, or "kinetic energy."

When Newton stated his laws of motion in the 1680's, he maintained that any object in motion would continue moving at the same velocity unless acted on by an outside force (see Chapter 7). In other words, a moving object's kinetic energy would always remain the same.

But in the real world, outside forces are always operating against moving objects and kinetic energy seems to disappear. A ball rolling along the ground slows and comes to a halt. A bouncing marble finally dribbles to a stop. A meteorite flashes through the air and is stopped by the earth.

What happens to the kinetic energy in all these cases? Some, but not all, of it may be converted to work. In fact, the bouncing marble and rolling ball may do no work at all and still their kinetic energy will disappear.

The Answer: Heat

The meteorite offers a hint. It creates a great deal of heat as it passes through the atmosphere — so much heat that it glows white hot.

Heat!

Enter an English scientist, James Prescott Joule
(JOWL). A rather sickly childhood had left Joule unable
to lead an active life, so he retired to the world of books
and became intrigued with science. Fortunately, he was
the son of a wealthy brewer who could afford to bring
the best tutors to his son. Joule eventually inherited the
brewery, but he always remained more interested in
science than in the world of business.

Joule's interest centered on the problem of the connec-
tion between energy and heat. He must have known about
Rumford's belief that heat was a form of motion. According to Rumford, heat consisted of the rapid motion
of tiny particles of matter (see Chapter 9).

If this were true, Joule saw, kinetic energy did not disappear at all. The motion of a rolling ball produced friction against the ground it rolled on. Friction produced
heat. Thus, the motion of the rolling ball was slowly converted to the motion of myriad particles — the particles
of the ball and those of the ground it touched.

Heat would then be another form of the energy of motion, Joule thought. Ordinary kinetic energy would be
turned into heat energy, with no loss. Perhaps this was
true of other forms of energy, too. It seemed to make
sense. Electricity and magnetism could do work, and so
could reactions between chemicals.

Thus there were electrical energy, magnetic energy,
and chemical energy. All could be turned into heat. For

instance, magnetism could produce an electric current that would heat a wire. And when coal burned, the chemical reaction of the coal and air could produce a great deal of heat.

Heat was just another form of these other kinds of energy, Joule reasoned. Therefore, a given quantity of energy always ought to produce a given quantity of heat. In 1840, as a young man of twenty-two, he began to make very careful and accurate measurements to test this possibility.

Joule stirred water or mercury with paddle wheels and measured the energy of the moving paddle wheels and the temperature rise in the liquid. He compressed air, then measured the energy that had gone into the compression and the heat that developed in the air. He forced water through narrow tubes. He produced an electric current in a coil of wire by rotating the coil between the poles of a magnet. He also passed a current through the wire without the help of a magnet. In each case, Joule measured the energy that was used up and the heat that appeared.

Even on his honeymoon he couldn't resist taking time out to measure the temperature at the top and bottom of a waterfall, to see how much heat had been produced by the energy of the falling water.

By 1847, Joule was satisfied that a given amount of energy of any sort always produced a given amount of heat. (Energy can be measured in units called ergs, and

heat is measured in calories.) Joule showed that one calorie of heat was produced whenever about 41,800,000
ergs of energy of any kind were used up. This relationship
between energy and heat is called the "mechanical equiva-
lent of heat." Later, a unit of energy called a joule was
established in Joule's honor. A joule is equal to 10,000,000
ergs; we can then say that one calorie equals 4.18 joules.

Reluctant Listeners

Joule had trouble announcing his discovery, for he was
neither a professor nor a member of any learned society.
He was just a brewer, and the scientists of the day would
not listen. Finally, Joule decided to give a public lecture
in Manchester — and then convinced a Manchester news-
paper to publish his lecture in full.

A few months later, he managed to make the same
speech before an audience of scientists, but they listened
coldly. They would have dismissed the whole subject,
except that a young man in the audience, William Thomson, rose to make points in sympathy with Joule. Thomson's comments were so shrewd and clever that the scientific audience could not help but take notice. (In later life
Thomson became one of the great scientists of the 19th
century. He is better known by the title Lord Kelvin.)

Thus, it was established that any form of energy could

be turned into only a fixed amount of heat. But heat itself was a form of energy. Might it not be that energy could never be destroyed or created? Might it not be that energy could only be converted from one form to another?

Misplaced Credit

In 1842, this idea occurred to a German scientist named Julius Robert Mayer. At that time, however, Joule's work had not been heard of and Mayer himself had made very few measurements. Mayer's belief seemed like something plucked out of thin air, and no one would pay any attention to him.

Another German scientist, Hermann Ludwig Ferdinand von Helmholtz made the same statement in 1847, apparently without knowing of Mayer's prior work. By this time Joule's work had been published. Scientists were at last ready to listen and, furthermore, to be impressed.

It is Helmholtz, therefore, who is usually given credit for what is known as "the law of conservation of energy." The simplest way of stating this law is as follows: *The total energy of the universe is constant.*

Mayer tried to remind the world that he had said the same thing in 1842, but everyone had forgotten or had never heard. Poor Mayer was accused of trying to steal credit. He was in such despair that he tried to kill himself by jumping out of a window. He survived, however, and lived in obscurity for thirty more years. It was only toward the end of his life that Julius Mayer's importance was realized.

The law of conservation of energy is often called "the first law of thermodynamics." Ever since the early part of the nineteenth century, scientists had been investigating the flow of heat from one object to another. This study is called "thermodynamics" (from Greek words meaning "motion of heat"). Once the law of conservation of energy was accepted, it had to be taken into account in all studies of thermodynamics.

Carnot's Engine

At the time that the law of conservation of energy was established, students of thermodynamics already realized that energy could not always be completely turned into work. Some of it always dribbled away as heat, no matter how they tried to stop it.

The first to show this by careful scientific analysis was a young French physicist, Nicholas Leonard Sadi Carnot. In 1824, he published a small book on the steam engine. In it he presented arguments to show that the heat energy turned out by a steam engine could not produce more than a certain amount of work. The amount of work depended on the difference in temperature between the hottest part of the steam engine and the coldest. If the entire steam engine were at one temperature, it would produce no work — no matter how much heat it built up.

Once Helmholtz had announced the law of conservation of energy, scientists turned back to Carnot's proofs of the limited work they could get out of a steam engine. Why was the work usually so much less than the energy produced by the engine? Temperature differences affected the work obtained, yes — Carnot had shown brilliantly that this was so — but why?

Clausius' Ratio

In 1850, the German physicist Rudolf Julius Emmanuel Clausius (KLOW-zee-oos) worked out the mathematics of the phenomenon. He did that by means of the concept of *absolute temperature*, or the temperature above *absolute zero*. No heat is present at absolute zero, that is, at —460 degrees Fahrenheit or —273 degrees centigrade.

Clausius found that if he divided the total heat energy of a system by its absolute temperature, he obtained a ratio that always increased in any natural process — whether the process was the burning of coal in a steam-engine system or hydrogen and helium exploding in the sun's "system." The more rapidly that ratio increased, the less work could be obtained from heat. By 1865 Clausius had named this ratio "entropy."

Does entropy increase in every natural process? It does. For example, it increases when cold objects warm up, when hot objects cool, when water pours downhill, when iron rusts, when meat decays, and so on. Nowadays the fact that entropy always increases is called "the second law of thermodynamics." This law can be expressed more simply as follows: *The total entropy of the universe is always increasing.*

The first and second laws of thermodynamics are perhaps the most fundamental statements yet made by scientists. No one has ever found exceptions; perhaps no one ever will. As nearly as we can tell, the laws apply to the entire universe, from the largest collections of stars to the smallest subatomic particles known.

Despite the revolutions that scientific thinking has undergone in the last century, the laws of thermodynamics have held firm. They remain a secure foundation for all of physical science.

11

Planck and Quanta

In the mid-nineteenth century science discovered that light provided each chemical element with a "set of fingerprints." How could light be used to distinguish one element from another?

If an element is heated until it glows, the light it emits will be made up of waves of various lengths. The group of wave lengths the element produces will be different from that of any other element.

Each individual wave length produces a different effect on the eye and is thus seen as a different color. Suppose that the light from a given element is separated into its various waves. The element's unique group of wave lengths should then show up as a unique pattern of colors. But how can the light from a glowing element be broken up into individual waves?

One answer is to pass it through a slit and then through a triangular piece of glass called a prism. The prism bends each wave by a different amount, according to its length. In this way, the prism forms images of the slit in the particular colors associated with the element's wave lengths. The result: a spectrum (plural, spectra) of colored lines whose pattern is different from that of any other element.

This procedure was worked out in detail in 1859 by a German physicist, Gustav Robert Kirchhoff (KIRKH-hof). He and the German chemist Robert Wilhelm von Bunsen invented the spectroscope — the instrument described above — and used it to study the spectra of various elements. They discovered two new elements when they found patterns unlike the spectrum of any known element.

Later, other scientists found the patterns of earthly elements in the spectra of the sun and the stars. On the other hand, the element helium was discovered in the sun in 1868, many years before it was detected on earth. These spectra studies finally demonstrated that the same matter made up all the universe.

Kirchhoff's most important finding was this: When a given element was heated until it gave off light of certain wave lengths, the element tended to absorb those same wave lengths of light when it was a bit cooler.

Black Body Concept

If an object absorbed all the light that fell on it, there would be none left to reflect. For this reason, it would appear black. Such an object could be called a "black body."

What ought to happen when such a black body is heated until it glows? According to Kirchhoff's finding it should give off light of every possible wave length, since it has absorbed them all. It happens that there are far more wave lengths in the invisible ultraviolet end of the electromagnetic spectrum (the system of all possible wave lengths of energy) than in all of the visible spectrum (the wave lengths that produce visible light). It would therefore seem that if a black body could radiate light of all wave lengths, most of the light would come from the violet and ultraviolet end of the spectrum.

In the 1890's an English physicist, Lord Rayleigh, worked out an equation based on the way light was then thought to behave. His results seemed to show that the shorter the wave length, the more light should be emitted. The shortest wave lengths of light were in the violet and ultraviolet end of the spectrum. Thus, the light should come off a black body in one quick flash of violet and ultraviolet — a "violet catastrophe."

But a violet catastrophe had never been observed. Why not? Perhaps because no ordinary object truly absorbs all the light that falls on it. If so, no object can be called a true black body, although physicists work with such bodies in theory. Perhaps if a true black body really existed, the violet catastrophe could be observed.

About the same time that Rayleigh's equation was worked out, the German physicist Wilhelm Wien (VEEN) thought he knew a way to produce a black body. He used a chamber with a small hole in it. Light of any wave length entering the hole, he thought, would be absorbed by the rough inner wall of the chamber. If part of the light was reflected, it would strike another portion of the inner wall and be absorbed there.

Once the light entered, it should not survive to emerge again from the hole. The hole would be a total absorber and would therefore act as a true black body. If the chamber was then heated until its interior glowed, the light that radiated out of the hole should be black body radiation.

Did the light radiate as a violet catastrophe?

Unfortunately, it didn't. Wien studied the radiation

that did emerge and found that it grew more intense as the wave lengths shortened (just as Rayleigh's equation predicted). There was always some particular wave length where radiation was most intense. But after that, the intensity of radiation would decline, although the wave lengths continued to shorten. The hotter Wien heated the chamber, the shorter the wave length after which the decline of radiation intensity began, but there was never a violet catastrophe.

Wien tried to work out an equation that described how the short and long wave lengths of light were radiated by his "black body," but the results were unsatisfactory.

In 1899 the problem was tackled by another German physicist, Max Planck. Perhaps light was radiated only in fixed amounts, he supposed. He didn't know how large those amounts might be, so he called them *quanta* (singular, *quantum*), from a Latin word meaning "how much?"

Up until then, all forms of energy, including light, were believed to exist in quantities as small as could be imagined. But Planck was suggesting that this was not so. He suggested instead that energy, like matter, existed only as particles of certain size. There could not be smaller quantities of energy than those he called quanta. Thus, quanta were "packets" of energy, just as atoms and molecules were "packets" of matter.

Planck supposed that a quantum of energy would vary in size according to the wave length of the light — the shorter the wave length, the larger the quantum. He applied this idea to the problem of black bodies and supposed them to be radiating light waves in the form of quanta. It would be easy for a black body to gather enough energy to make small quanta. Therefore, it could easily radiate long wave lengths of light, which required smaller quanta. But a short wave length could not be radiated unless large quanta were gathered. It would be much more difficult for a black body to gather these large quanta.

It is as though you were in a large store and were told you could buy anything at all, provided you paid cash in coin for it. It would be easy for you to buy a ten-cent item. But you would have a great deal of trouble buying a thousand-dollar item because you probably would find it impossible to carry so many coins.

Planck succeeded in working out an equation to describe black body radiation in terms of quanta. The equation backed up Wien's observation that there was some wave length at which radiation would be most intense. For wave lengths shorter than that, the black body would have difficulty in producing the larger quanta necessary.

But, if the black body chamber were heated to higher temperatures, more energy would be available. Therefore, shorter wave lengths made up of larger quanta could be produced.

However, there would always be a wave length that was too short, even for a strongly heated black body. It would then be impossible to emit the very large quanta required. Therefore, there could never be a violet catastrophe. In much the same way, there would always be something too expensive for the amount of coins you could carry.

Planck's "quantum theory" was announced in 1900, but it did not make much of a splash at first. However, physicists were already setting the stage for such a "splash" as they began to study the peculiar behavior of particles smaller than atoms (subatomic particles).

Some of this behavior could not be explained with existing knowledge. For instance, when light fell on certain metals, why did tiny subatomic particles, called "electrons," behave the way they did? The light was able to eject electrons from atoms on the surface of the metals. But these electrons were ejected only if the wave lengths of light falling on the metals were shorter than a certain value. That value depended on the nature of the metal. How were physicists going to explain this phenomenon, which was called the "photoelectric effect"?

In 1905 Albert Einstein came up with the answer. He used the quantum theory to explain the photoelectric effect. When long wave lengths of light fell on a given metal, the quanta of these wave lengths would be too small to knock out any electrons, Einstein suggested. However, as the wave lengths grew shorter and shorter, the quanta would become large enough to eject electrons.

Thus, Einstein explained why electrons weren't ejected until the wave length of the light shining on the metal was shorter than a certain critical amount.

The answer to the puzzle of the photoelectric effect was a great victory for the quantum theory, and both Planck and Einstein eventually were awarded Nobel prizes for their work.

The quantum theory again proved its value in research on the structure of the atom. Physicists had decided that the atom consisted of a relatively massive central nucleus around which one or more electrons moved in circular paths, or orbits. According to the physical theories of the time, the electrons should have radiated light as they circled, lost energy, and collapsed into the nucleus of the atom. But electrons kept on circling the nucleus and did not collapse into it. It was obvious that the older theories could not explain the motion of electrons.

In 1913, however, the Danish physicist Niels Bohr (BAWR) applied the quantum theory to atomic structure. Bohr said that an electron could emit energy only in fixed amounts, that is, in whole quanta. As the energy was emitted, the electron would take up a new orbit closer to the nucleus of the atom. Correspondingly, the electron could absorb only whole quanta, taking up a new orbit farther from the nucleus. The electron could never collapse into the nucleus, for it could never come closer than the closest orbit permitted by its energy state.

Answers and Understanding

By considering the different orbits allowable, physicists were able to understand why each element radiated only certain wave lengths of light, and why the light absorbed was always the same as the light emitted. In this way Kirchhoff's rule, which started it all, was finally explained.

Then in 1927 the Austrian physicist Erwin Schrödinger (SHROI-ding-er) worked out the mathematics of the atom according to quantum mechanics. Schrödinger's explanation took in practically every aspect of the study of the atom, and his work is crucial to atomic research. In fact, even the way in which the atom stores and releases energy couldn't possibly be understood without it.

Quantum mechanics is now so important that modern physics is considered to date only from Planck's announcement of the quantum theory in 1900. Physics before 1900 is called classical physics. Planck's relatively simple idea succeeded in changing completely the direction of the science of matter and motion.

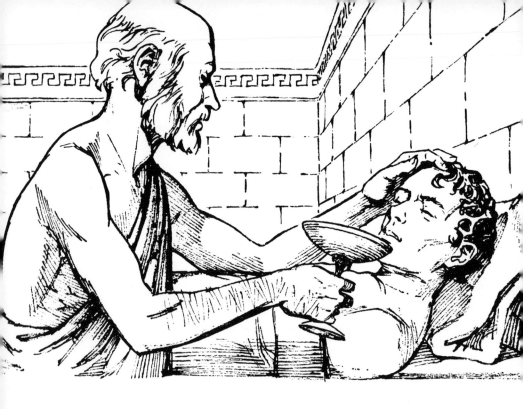

12

Hippocrates and Medicine

How WONDERFUL the miracle of life is, and how amazing living things are! The smallest plant or animal seems more complicated, more intriguing, than the largest mass of nonliving matter imaginable.

Nonliving matter, after all, seems to do nothing at all most of the time. Or if it does do something, it does so in a mechanical and rather uninteresting way. Consider a rock lying in the road. If nothing disturbs it, it will just lie there forever. If you kick it, it will move and then stop. Kick it harder and it will move farther. If you throw it up in the air, it will move in a curve of a particular shape and come down. And if you hit it with a sledge hammer, it will break.

With a little experience you can predict exactly what will happen to a rock when any given thing is done to it. You can describe what happens in terms of *cause and effect*. If a particular thing is done to a rock (a cause), a particular thing will happen to the rock as a result (an effect). The belief that the same cause will bring about the same effect every time leads to a view of the universe, called the "mechanical view," or "mechanism" (see Chapter 8).

Predictable Universe

Even something as remarkable as the sun seems to rise mechanically every morning and set mechanically every evening. If you watch it carefully, you can learn to predict exactly when it will rise and set every day of the year, as well as exactly what part of the sky it will cross. The ancients worked out rules to predict the motion of the sun and the other heavenly bodies, and the rules they formulated were never broken.

About 600 B.C. the Greek philosopher Thales and his followers stated their belief that the "natural law" of cause and effect was all that was needed to understand nature (see Chapter 1). Such natural law made it unnecessary to suppose that spirits or demons ruled the universe.

But could this natural law be applied to living things? Weren't living things a rule unto themselves, and didn't they often fail to follow the law of cause and effect?

Uncertain Result

Suppose you push a friend. He might fall down or he might manage to keep his balance. After you had pushed him he might laugh or call you names, or push you in return — or he might angrily try to strike you. He might even do nothing at all or he might do nothing for a while and try to get back at you later. In other words, a living thing may respond to a particular cause with any number of effects. This belief that living creatures don't obey the rules that govern the nonliving universe is called "vitalism."

Then, too, consider that some men have unusual abilities. Why is it that one man can write beautiful poetry while another cannot? Why is one man a clever leader, or an inspiring speaker, or a brave warrior, while others are not?

On the other hand, all men seem to be basically alike.

All have arms and legs, ears and eyes, hearts and brains. Then what makes the difference between an unusual and an ordinary man?

To the ancients, a man might be unusual because he was favored by some personal spirit or guardian angel. The Greeks called such spirit a *daimon,* and that became our word "demon." We still say that someone who works a great deal seems to be "possessed by demons."

Similarly, the word "enthusiastic," which means "unusually interested in something," comes from a Greek expression meaning "possessed by a god." A man who does great work is said to be "inspired," which is from a Latin word meaning "to breathe in" — that is, to draw into oneself an invisible spirit. And the word "genius" is from the Latin version of the Greek word *daimon.*

Naturally, these spirits and demons were expected to work evil for man as well as good. If a man became ill, the ancients said he was possessed by an evil spirit. The belief seemed most valid when a man began to say and do foolish things. No man would willingly act foolish, so people blamed "the demon within him." Therefore, in primitive societies the mentally ill were sometimes treated with awe and respect. The madman was considered to have been touched by the finger of some supernatural being (and we still use the word "touched" to described someone who seems not quite in his right mind).

The "Sacred Disease"

The disease epilepsy, which we now know to be a disorder of the brain, also seemed to be caused by a spirit. Occasionally, a person with this disorder loses control of his body for a few minutes. He might fall down (for this reason, the disease was called the "falling sickness"), thrash about, and so on. Afterward, he remembers very little of what happened. People watching such an occurrence in ancient times were sure they saw a demon enter the stricken person's body and throw it about. The Greeks therefore referred to epilepsy as the "sacred disease."

As long as illness was looked on in this unscientific way, the method of treating it was bound to be just as unscientific. To coax or frighten away the demons was considered the proper method of treatment. Primitive tribes still have "witch doctors" to cast spells and perform rites that are supposed to make the evil spirits leave a sick person. The people believe that the sick person will get well as soon as the evil spirits have been cast out.

The Greeks had a god of medicine, called Asklepios (as-KLEP-ee-os), and the priests of Asklepios were doctors. On the Greek island of Kos, in the Aegean Sea (just off the western coast of modern Turkey), stood an important temple of Asklepios. About 400 B.C. the greatest doctor on the island of Kos was a man named Hippocrates (hih-POK-ruh-teez).

Hippocrates' view point was new to the Greeks, for he believed in treating the patient rather than worrying about the demon inside him. He was not the first in history to do so. The old civilizations in Babylonia and Egypt must have had many doctors who took this attitude, and there is a legend that Hippocrates studied in Egypt. But it is the work of Hippocrates that has survived and it is his name that is remembered.

A Sensible School

Hippocrates established a school that continued for centuries. The doctor of his school used common sense in treating patients. They didn't have modern medicines, equipment, or theories. But they did have common sense and the ability to observe things keenly.

Hippocrates' followers believed that doctors should keep their patients — and themselves — clean. They thought the sick should have fresh air, comfortable and restful surroundings, and a balanced diet of simple food. They worked out sensible rules for stopping bleeding, for cleaning and treating wounds, for setting broken bones, and so on. All extremes were avoided, and all magical rites were ignored.

The writings of the entire Hippocratic school are lumped together, and it is impossible to tell exactly who wrote a particular part or when it was written. The best known of these Hippocratic writings is an oath taken by each doctor of the school as he prepared to enter his profession. Because the oath upholds the highest ideals of medical practice, it is still used as a guide for physicians. Medical school students recite it when they are graduated. The "Hippocratic oath" was not written by Hippocrates, however. The best guess is that it came into use about 200 A.D., six centuries after Hippocrates lived.

Is there any Hippocratic writing that we can attribute to Hippocrates himself? There *is* one treatise among the oldest of these writings that may well have been written by Hippocrates. It is called "On the Sacred Disease" and it deals with epilepsy.

Demons Dismissed

This treatise strongly maintains that it is useless to blame demons for disease. Every disease has some natural cause, and it is the task of the doctor to discover it. Once the cause is known, the cure may be found. And this is true, the treatise states, even of that mysterious and frightening disease epilepsy. It is not a sacred disease at all, but a sickness like any other.

What the treatise says, in effect, is that the idea of cause and effect applies to living things, including man. Because living things are so complicated, it may not be simple to trace cause and effect relations. But in the end it can — and must — be done.

Medicine had to struggle for many more centuries against the common belief in demons and evil spirits, and against the use of magical rites and spells as cures. But the views of Hippocrates were never entirely forgotten.

Because of Hippocrates' ideas on the treatment of the sick, he is often called the "father of medicine." Actually, he is even more than that. He applied the notion of natural law to living things and thus took the first great step against vitalism. Once natural law was applied to life, scientists could begin to study it systematically. Hippocrates' view therefore made a science of life (biology) possible, and he may also be considered the "father of biology."

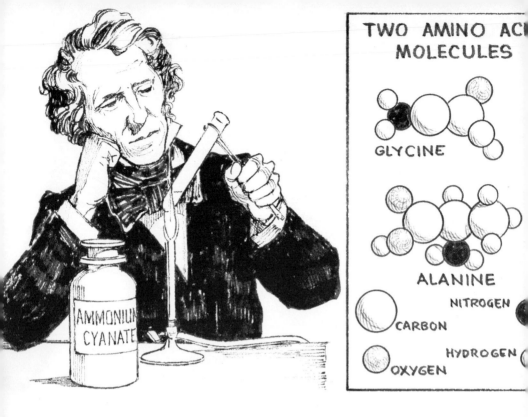

TWO AMINO ACI
MOLECULES

GLYCINE

ALANINE

NITROGEN

CARBON

HYDROGEN

OXYGEN

AMMONIUM CYANATE

13

Wöhler and Organic Chemistry

In 1828 a young German chemist, Friedrich Wöhler
(VOL-ler), knew exactly where his interests lay — in
studying metals and minerals. Such substances belonged to
the field of inorganic chemistry, which dealt with substances that supposedly had nothing to do with life. There
was also organic chemistry, dealing with chemicals that
formed in the tissues of living plants and animals.

Wöhler's teacher, the Swedish chemist Jöns J. Berzelius (ber-ZEE-lee-us), had divided chemistry into these two classifications. Berzelius insisted further that organic chemicals couldn't be formed from inorganic chemicals in the laboratory. They could be formed only in living tissue because they required some "vital force."

Vitalist View

Berzelius was a vitalist, a believer in "vitalism" (see Chapter 12). He believed that living matter followed laws of nature different from those followed by nonliving matter. More than two thousand years earlier, Hippocrates had suggested that the same laws of nature held for both. But that was still hard to believe, since living tissue was so complicated and its functions so hard to understand. Many chemists were therefore sure that the simple methods of the laboratory would never do for the complex substances found in living organisms.

So Wöhler worked with inorganic chemicals, never dreaming he was about to revolutionize the field of organic chemistry. It all began with an inorganic chemical called ammonium cyanate. When Wöhler heated it, it changed into another substance. In order to identify the substance, Wöhler studied its properties. As factor after factor checked out, he grew increasingly astonished.

To play it safe, he repeated the experiment again and again, but the result was always the same. Ammonium cyanate, an inorganic substance, had turned into urea, a well-known organic compound. Wöhler had done something Berzelius considered impossible: He had formed an organic substance from an inorganic one simply by heating it!

Wöhler's pioneering discovery was a revelation, and other chemists tried to make organic compounds out of inorganic ones. One French chemist, Pierre E. Berthelot (behr-teh-LOH), made dozens of such compounds in the 1850's. At the same time an English chemist, William H. Perkin, was forming a substance that resembled organic compounds in its properties, but was not to be found anywhere in the realm of life. Thousands and tens of thousands of such synthetic organic compounds followed.

Chemists could now make compounds that nature formed only in living tissue. Furthermore, they could also make additional compounds of the same sort that living tissues could not produce!

However, these facts did not wipe out vitalistic explanations. Chemists might be able to produce the same compounds made by living tissue, but hardly in the same manner, the vitalists said. Living tissue produced its substances under conditions of mild temperature and with only the most gentle substances. The chemist had to use considerable heat, or pressure, or strong chemicals.

But chemists did know how to cause certain reactions at room temperature that ordinarily would take place only with heat. The trick was to use a *catalyst*. Powdered platinum, for instance, would cause hydrogen to burst into flame as it mixed with air. Without the platinum, heat was required to bring on the reaction.

Catalysts of Life

It therefore seemed clear that living tissue had to contain catalysts, but catalysts of no kind known to man. The catalysts of living tissue were extremely efficient. A tiny amount would bring about a large reaction. They were also extremely selective. Their presence would cause particular substances to undergo changes, while very similar substances would not be affected.

Then, too, the catalysts of life were easily put out of action. Heat, strong chemicals, or small quantities of certain metals or other substances would stop their action, usually for good.

These catalysts of life were called "ferments." The best-known examples were the ferments in the tiny yeast cells. Since the dawn of history, man had used these ferments to make wine from fruit juices and to make soft, puffy breads from flat cakes of dough.

In 1752 a French scientist, René A. F. de Réaumur

(ray-oh-MYOOR), obtained some stomach juices from a hawk and showed that the juices could dissolve meat. But how? The juice itself was not living.

Chemists shrugged. The answer seemed easy enough. There were two kinds of ferments. One kind worked outside the living cells to digest food. Those were "unorganized" ferments. Then there were "organized" ferments, which could work only inside living cells. The ferments in yeast, which broke down sugars and starches to form wine or raise bread, were examples of organized ferments.

By the middle 1800's the old vitalism had been discredited, thanks to the work of Wöhler and his successors. But a new form of vitalism had taken its place. The new vitalists said living processes could take place only as a result of the action of organized ferments, which could exist only inside living cells. They said the organized ferments were in fact the "life force."

In 1876 a German chemist, Wilhelm Kühne (KYOO-nuh), insisted that the digestive juices not be called unorganized ferments. The word "ferment" was so associated with life, it might give the impression that a living process was taking place outside the cells. Instead, Kühne suggested that the digestive juices be said to contain *enzymes*. The word "enzyme," from a Greek expression meaning "in yeast," seemed appropriate because the digestive juices behaved somewhat like the ferments in yeast.

Exit Vitalism

The new vitalism had to be tested. If ferments worked only in living cells, then anything that killed the cell should destroy the ferment. To be sure, when yeast cells were killed, they stopped fermenting. But perhaps they weren't killed in the right way. Usually, they were killed by heat or by strong chemicals. Could something else be substituted?

It occurred to a German chemist, Eduard Buchner, that yeast cells might be killed by grinding them with sand. The fine, hard particles of sand would rupture the tiny cells and destroy them. But the ferments inside would not be exposed to heat or to chemicals. Would they be destroyed anyway?

In 1896 Buchner ground yeast and filtered it. He studied the juices under the microscope and was certain that not one living yeast cell was present in it. It was just "dead" juice. He then added a solution of sugar. Bubbles of carbon dioxide began to come off at once, and the sugar slowly turned to alcohol.

Chemists now knew that "dead" juice could carry out a process which they had thought impossible without living cells. This time vitalism was really smashed. All ferments, inside and outside the cell, were alike. Kühne's word "enzyme," which he had used only for ferments outside the cell, came to be used for all ferments.

Therefore, by the twentieth century most chemists had decided that there were no mysterious forces inside living cells. Whatever processes took place in tissues were performed by means of ordinary chemicals. Such chemicals could be worked with in test tubes if delicate and gentle enough laboratory methods were used.

Isolating an Enzyme

However, scientists had yet to determine exactly what chemicals made up the enzymes. But enzymes were present in such small traces that they were almost impossible to isolate and identify.

In 1926 the American biochemist James B. Sumner showed the way. He was working with an enzyme present in the juice of mashed jack beans. When crystals formed in the juice, Sumner isolated them. In solution, they produced a very active enzyme reaction. Anything that destroyed the molecular structure of the crystals destroyed the enzyme action. Nor could Sumner separate the enzyme action from the crystals.

Sumner had to conclude that the crystals were the enzyme. For the first time an enzyme had been obtained in a clearly visible form. Further testing proved the crystals to consist of *protein*. Since then, many enzymes have been crystallized, and without exception they have proved to be proteins.

A String of Acids

Proteins have a molecular structure that is now well understood. In the nineteenth century proteins were found to consist of twenty different kinds of smaller units named "amino acids." In 1907 a German chemist, Emil Fischer, showed how amino acids were strung together in a protein molecule.

In the 1950's and 1960's a number of chemists, particularly an Englishman named Frederick Sanger, succeeded in pulling protein molecules apart. In this way they were able to determine exactly which amino acid went where in the molecule. In addition, some simple protein molecules were artificially formed in the laboratory.

Hippocrates' nonvitalistic view has thus been supported by more than a century and a half of painstaking scientific work. This careful search for truth has uncovered the life processes of a cell and has shown that cell components are only chemicals, not "ferments" or other vitalistic forces. Thus, from Wöhler to Sanger, scientists have proved that the natural laws of the universe govern living, as well as nonliving, matter.

14

Linnaeus and Classification

Perhaps the most influential scientific mind in the history of the world was that of the Greek philosopher Aristotle (384 B.C. to 322 B.C.).

Aristotle was probably the best known pupil at Plato's Academy in Athens. A few years after Plato's death in 347 B.C., Aristotle went to the kingdom of Macedon, in northern Greece, where his father had been court physician. There he spent several years as tutor to the young Macedonian prince Alexander, who was to become Alexander the Great.

When Alexander left on his carer of conquest, Aristotle returned to Athens and established a school of his own. His teachings were collected into what was almost a one-man encyclopedia of ancient thought and knowledge. Many of these books survived and were considered the last word in scientific thinking for nearly two thousand years.

Influential — but Wrong

The influence of Aristotle's ideas on later scientists was considerable, particularly his views on the nature of the universe, on the movement of objects, and so on (see Chapters 4 and 7). In the area of physical science, however, he was usually wrong.

Aristotle's views on biological subjects were less influential, but he was actually strongest in this area. Natural science was his favorite subject, and he spent years studying the animals of the sea.

Aristotle was not satisfied simply to look at animals and describe them. With his clear mind and his love of order, he went further and classified animals into groups. Such classification is now called "taxonomy," which comes from Greek words meaning "a system of arrangement."

All of us have a tendency to classify things. We can see that lions and tigers closely resemble each other, that sheep resemble goats, that houseflies resemble horseflies. But Aristotle was not content with such casual observations. He listed more than five hundred different kinds of animals and carefully grouped all of them into classes. What's more, he arranged these classes in order, from the very simplest to the most complex.

He noted that some animals did not belong to the class which they seemed to resemble most. For instance, almost everybody took it for granted that the dolphin was a fish. It lived in the water and was shaped like a fish. But Aristotle observed that the dolphin breathed air, that it brought forth living young, and that it nourished the young before birth with an organ called a "placenta." In these respects the dolphin resembled the four-legged beasts of the dry land, and Aristotle therefore considered it a mammal rather than a fish.

Aristotle was absolutely right, but naturalists ignored his conclusion for two thousand years. Aristotle seemed fated to be believed when he was wrong and disbelieved when he was right.

Naturalists who came after Aristotle did not carry on his efforts to classify animals. In ancient and medieval times books describing animals arranged them in any order and ignored the possibility of grouping together animals with similar structures.

In the 1500's, however, naturalists made the first attempts at such classification since Aristotle. But these attempts were not very thorough. For example, one writer might group together all plants with narrow leaves while another might do the same for all plants with big yellow flowers.

The first naturalist to do as thorough a job as Aristotle was an Englishman named John Ray. Ray traveled through Europe, studying plants and animals. In 1667 and for thirty-five years thereafter he published books that described and classified the plants and animals he had studied.

He began to classify mammals by dividing them into two main groups — those with toes and those with hooves. Then he went on to subdivide these classifications according to the number of hooves or toes, according to whether the toes bore claws or nails, and according to whether a hooved animal had permanent horns or horns that were shed. Thus, Ray restored the sense of order that Aristotle had brought to the realm of life.

Once Ray had shown the way, naturalists soon went beyond Aristotle. In 1735 a young Swedish naturalist named Carl von Linné published a small book in which he listed different creatures according to a system of his own. (He is better known by the Latin version of his name,

Carolus Linnaeus [li-NEE-us].) He based his work on extensive travel throughout Europe (including northern Scandinavia, which had never before been adequately explored).

Linnaeus briefly and clearly described each kind, or *species* (plural, also *species*), of plant and animal. He grouped each collection of similar species into a *genus* (plural, *genera*). Then he gave each kind of plant or animal two Latin names — one for its genus and one for its species.

For example, the cat and the lion are two species that are very much alike, even though one is so much larger and fiercer than the other. Hence, both are in the same genus, the genus *Felis* (Latin for "cat"). A second Latin name serves to distinguish the ordinary cat from the lion and from other species of the genus. Thus, the cat is *Felis domesticus*, while the lion is *Felis leo*.

Similarly, the dog and the wolf are both in the genus *Canis* ("dog"). The dog is *Canis familiaris* and the wolf is *Canis lupus*.

Linnaeus even gave human beings such a Latin name. He placed man in the genus *Homo* ("man") and called the human species *Homo sapiens* ("man, wise").

Linnaeus' system is known as "binomial nomenclature." Actually, we use a similar system to identify ourselves. In America, everyone in the same family has a particular family name, but different first names. Thus, one brother might be listed in the telephone directory as "Anderson, George," and another as "Anderson, William."

Linnaeus' work was tremendously useful. For the first time, naturalists the world over had a common system of names to identify different creatures. Whenever any naturalist spoke of *Canis lupus,* other naturalists knew immediately he meant a wolf. It made no difference what language they spoke or what familiar name "wolf" might have in their own language. What's more, they knew the naturalist meant one particular kind of wolf, the European gray wolf. The American timber wolf, for example, was a different species, *Canis occidentalis.*

This common system of identification was a very important step forward. As man explored the earth and discovered new continents, he found more and more species of animals. Aristotle had listed only about five hundred species, but by Linnaeus' time tens of thousands were known.

Linnaeus' book of animal classification started off with only seven pages in its first edition, but expanded to two thousand five hundred pages by its tenth. If naturalists had not adopted a standard classification system, they could not have been certain as to which plants or animals other naturalists were discussing. The study of natural history would have collapsed in chaos.

From genus and species classification, Linnaeus went on to group similar genera into *orders,* and similar orders into *classes.* Linnaeus recognized six different classes of animals: mammals, birds, reptiles, fish, insects, and worms.

His work was carried still further by a French biologist, Georges Cuvier (koo-VYAY). Cuvier saw that the first four classes — mammals, birds, reptiles, and fish — were all *vertebrates;* that is, all had internal skeletons of bone. He grouped these animals into a still larger classification called a "phylum" (plural, "phyla"). Cuvier and the French naturalist Jean Baptiste de Lamarck divided the *invertebrates*, or animals without internal skeletons, into a number of phyla.

Cuvier moved taxonomy in another direction, too. After 1800 naturalists began studying rocks with stony impressions or remnants that seemed to have been living creatures. They called these impressions or remnants "fossils." Cuvier recognized that although fossils did not closely resemble any existing species, they did fall somewhere into the scheme of taxonomy.

For instance, when Cuvier studied a fossil that had all the earmarks of a reptile skeleton, he concluded that the animal had been a member of the class of reptiles. From its skeleton he could also tell that it once had wings. Cuvier had thus identified the first of a group of extinct flying reptiles. Because each of its wings had been supported by a single long finger bone, he named the creature "pterodactyl" ("wing-finger").

Pathway to Evolution

Cuvier's followers continued to improve the system of classification. Linnaeus had often grouped animals together on the basis of outward appearances. Instead, Cuvier's followers began to use internal structures, which were more important for grouping purposes.

By the middle 1800's a system for classifying all living things had been worked out. The work that Aristotle had begun so long ago had finally been completed. Every creature, alive or extinct, could be placed in a particular category. There might be disputes about some of the fine details, but the general plan was accepted.

The development of taxonomy set naturalists thinking. The fact that life could be classified so neatly suggested that there must be certain biological principles that held true for all creatures, however different they might appear.

Thus, the classification of life gave rise to the idea that all living things were involved in some single phenomenon. This idea, in turn, was to lead to one of the overwhelming "great ideas of science" — *evolution* (see Chapter 15).

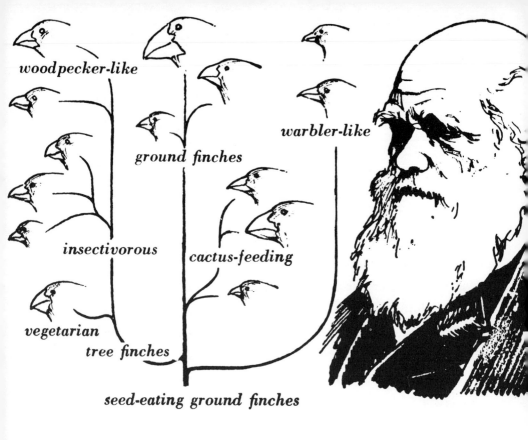

woodpecker-like

ground finches

warbler-like

insectivorous

cactus-feeding

vegetarian
tree finches

seed-eating ground finches

15

Darwin and Evolution

THERE'S SOMETHING special about being a lion, a cat, or a
rose — something that no other animal or plant can share.
Each one is a unique species, or kind, of animal or plant.
Only lions can give birth to baby lions, only cats can have
kittens, and only rose seeds — and not dandelion seeds —
can come up roses.

Still, it is possible for two different species to show similarities. Lions are much like tigers, for example, and jackals are much like coyotes — even though lions breed only lions and not tigers, and jackals breed jackals and not coyotes.

In fact, the whole realm of life can be conveniently organized into groups of similar creatures (see Chapter 14). When scientists first became aware of this, many felt that these similarities could not be just a coincidence. Were two species alike because members of one species had changed into the other? Could it be that different species resembled each other simply because they were closely related?

Some of the Greek philosophers had suggested the possibility of relationship between species, but their suggestion had seemed too outlandish and fell on deaf ears. It seemed unlikely that some lions had once turned into tigers or vice versa, or that some catlike creature had given rise to both lions and tigers. No one had ever seen such a thing happen. Therefore, if it happened at all, it must have been a very slow process.

In early modern times most people were convinced that the earth was only about six thousand years old. Thus, there simply was not enough time for species to have changed their nature. The whole idea was dismissed as absurd.

But was the earth really only six thousand years old? In

the 1700's scientists studying the structure of the rocky layers of the earth's crust were beginning to suspect that those layers could be formed only over long periods of time. About 1760 a French naturalist, Georges de Buffon (byoo-FONG), was daring enough to suggest that the earth might be as much as seventy-five thousand years old.

Then, in 1785, a Scottish physician named James Hutton went further. Hutton, who had developed his hobby of studying rocks into a full-time occupation, published a book called *The Theory of the Earth*. In it he brought together much evidence and many good arguments to show that the earth might actually be many millions of years old. He said firmly that he saw no sign of any beginning at all.

The Door Opens

For the first time it seemed possible to talk about the *evolution* of life. If the earth was millions of years old, there would have been enough time for animals and plants to change very slowly into new species — so slowly, in fact, that man could not have noticed this evolution in the few thousand years of his civilized existence.

But why should a species change at all? And why should it change in one particular direction and not in another? The first person to attempt to answer that question was the French naturalist Jean Baptiste de Lamarck.

In 1809 he presented his theory of evolution in a book entitled *Zoological Philosophy*. The theory suggested that creatures changed because they tried to change, without necessarily knowing what they were doing.

Lamarck hypothesized, for example, that a certain antelope was fond of browsing on the leaves of trees. It would stretch its neck upward with all its might to reach all the leaves it could. It would stretch its tongue and its legs, too. All this stretching throughout its life would cause its legs, neck, and tongue to lengthen slightly.

The antelope would then have young that would inherit those longer body proportions. The offspring would in turn lengthen their bodies still more by stretching. Little by little, over many thousands of years, the stretching would reach the point where that line of antelopes became a new species — the giraffe.

Lamarck's theory depended on the concept of *inheritance of acquired characteristics*. That is, if a creature's body changed during its lifetime, this change could be passed on to the young. However, there was no evidence to support such a concept. Indeed, as the possibility was investigated, it began to seem more and more that it could not be so. Lamarck's idea had to be abandoned.

In 1831 a young English naturalist named Charles Darwin joined the crew of a ship sent out to explore the world. Just before leaving, he had read a book on geology by an

Englishman, Charles Lyell. The book discussed and explained Hutton's theories about the age of the earth. Darwin was impressed.

As the ship passed distant coasts and explored little-known islands, Darwin had a chance to study species of creatures still unknown to Europeans. He was particularly interested in the animal life of the Galápagos Islands, located in the Pacific about 650 miles off the coast of Ecuador.

Darwin found fourteen different species of finches on those obscure islands. All differed slightly from one another, and from similar finches on the South American coast. The beaks of some finches were well designed for eating small seeds, and those of others for eating large ones. Other finches had beaks made for eating insects.

Darwin suspected that all the different finches originated from a common ancestor. What had made them change? An idea flashed through Darwin's mind. Perhaps some had been born with slight changes in their beaks and had passed such inborn characteristics on to their young. Darwin wasn't sure, though. Would such accidental changes be enough to account for the evolution of different species?

In 1838 Darwin found an answer in *An Essay on the Principle of Population*, a book published in 1798 by an English clergyman named Thomas R. Malthus. Malthus maintained that the human population always increased faster than its food supply. Therefore, the number of people eventually would be reduced by famine, if not by disease or war.

Nature's Way

Darwin was impressed by Malthus' arguments, for they made him see how powerful a force nature could exert — not only on the human population, but on the population of any species.

Many creatures multiply in great numbers, but only a small proportion ever survives. It seemed to Darwin that in general those that were more efficient in one way or another were the ones that survived. For example, those finches born with slightly stronger beaks would survive because they were better able to eat tough seeds. Those that could digest an occasional insect would have an even better chance of survival.

Generation after generation, the finches that were slightly more efficient in any way would survive at the expense of the slightly less efficient ones. There were a number of ways in which they might be more efficient. Therefore, in the end there would be a number of widely different species, each specializing in a different way.

It seemed to Darwin that this process of *natural selection* held true not only for finches, but for all creatures. Natural selection determined which creatures would survive by starving out those that did not have some little edge of superiority.

Darwin worked on his theory of natural selection for years. Finally, in 1859, he published his views in a book entitled *On the Origin of Species by Means of Natural Selection, or the Preservation of Favoured Races in the Struggle for Life.*

At first, Darwin's views created a storm of controversy. But more and more evidence gathered through the years has supported the central point of his theory — the slow change of species through natural selection.

The idea of evolution, first glimpsed by the Greek philosophers and finally nailed down by Charles Darwin, revolutionized all thinking in biology. It was undoubtedly the most important single idea in the history of modern biology.

16

Russell and Stellar Evolution

ARISTOTLE THOUGHT that the earth and the heavens ran
by different laws (see Chapter 7). On earth, he observed,
there was erratic change — sunshine and storm, growth
and decay. On the other hand, he believed that the
heavens never changed. The sun, moon, and planets circled
the heavens so mechanically that their position at any given

moment could be predicted long in advance. The stars remained always in place, always the same.

To be sure, there were objects which seemed to be falling stars, but to Aristotle they did not fall from the heavens. They were just phenomena in the air, and the air belonged to the earth. (We know that falling stars are rocks that enter the earth's atmosphere from outer space. The friction produced as they fall through the atmosphere causes them to burn and give off light. Thus, Aristotle was both wrong and right about falling stars. He was wrong because they *do* come from the heavens, but right because they *become* "things in the air." In fact, falling stars are also called "meteors," from a Greek word meaning "things in the air.")

In 134 B.C., two centuries after Aristotle's death, the Greek astronomer Hipparchus (hih-PAHR-kus) noted a new star in the constellation Scorpio. What was he to think? Could stars be "born"? Could the heavens change after all? But perhaps his observation was wrong, he thought. Perhaps the star had always been there.

To make sure that no future astronomer would be fooled, Hipparchus prepared a map of more than a thousand bright stars. It was the first star map, and the best for the next sixteen hundred years. However, no more new stars were reported for many centuries.

In 1054 A.D. a new star appeared in the constellation Taurus, but only Chinese and Japanese astronomers noted it. In Europe, science was at a low ebb — so low, in fact, that no astronomer reported the new star, although for weeks it blazed brighter than any object in the sky except for the sun and moon.

In 1572 a bright new star blazed up once again, this time in the constellation Cassiopeia. By this time, science was again beginning to flourish in Europe and astronomers were watching the heavens carefully. Among them was a young Dane named Tycho Brahe (BRAH-uh). He observed the star and wrote a book about it entitled *De Nova Stella* ("Concerning the New Star"). Ever since, a new star in the heavens has been called a "nova."

There was no denying it now. Aristotle had been wrong. The heavens were not changeless.

More Evidence of Change

More was in store. In 1577 a comet appeared in the heavens, and Brahe tried to calculate its distance from the earth. He did this by having its position noted against the stars — at as nearly the same time as possible — from two different observatories. The observatories were a considerable distance apart — one was in Denmark and the other in Czechoslovakia. Brahe knew that the comet should seem to shift position when seen from two different places. The closer it was to earth, the more it should shift.

However, the comet didn't shift at all; the moon shifted instead. This meant that the comet was farther away than the moon. Therefore, despite its erratic motion, the comet was a part of the heavens.

Then in 1596 the Dutch astronomer David Fabricius (fuh-BRISH-us) discovered a strange star in the constellation Cetus. The star was always changing its brightness. Sometimes it was very bright, sometimes so dim it could not be seen. It was a "variable star" and represented another kind of change. The star came to be called Mira ("wonderful").

Still other changes were observed. In 1718, for example, the English astronomer Edmund Halley showed that some stars had indeed changed their positions since Greek times.

Without a doubt, there were many kinds of changes in the heavens. But was it possible to make sense of them or were they just random changes?

An answer to this question became possible after the German physicist Gustav R. Kirchhoff invented the spectroscope on 1859 (see also Chapter 11). A spectroscope is a device that splits any light falling on it into a pattern, or spectrum, of colors. Each chemical element emitting light has its own spectrum. Therefore, the spectroscope can identify the elements in a source of light and has been used to determine those elements present in the sun and in other stars.

Different stars produce different "light spectra." In

1867 an Italian astronomer, Pietro A. Secchi (SAYK-kee), divided stars into four different "spectral classes." Later astronomers divided them more finely, into ten classes.

This was an exciting development, for it meant that stars could not be classified in groups according to their properties, just as plants and animals could be classified according to their characteristics (see Chapter 14).

In 1893 the German physicist Wilhelm Wien showed how the light emitted by any source varied with its temperature. Wien's work made it possible to tell the surface temperature of a star just from its spectral class. It turned out that the temperature seemed to be related to the color and size of the star.

The Danish astronomer Ejnar Hertzsprung (in 1905) and the American astronomer Henry N. Russell (in 1914) compared the temperatures of various stars to their *luminosity* (the amount of light given off). They plotted graphs of the results and found that almost all the stars fell into a straight line which came to be called "the main sequence."

There were cool, red stars — huge bodies known as "red giants." Although each part of their surface was dim, they gave off a lot of light because the total surface was very great.

Then there were yellow stars, hotter than the red giants. Although smaller, they still could be called "yellow giants." There were still smaller and hotter stars — hot

enough to be blue-white. Blue-white stars appeared to
have the maximum temperature. After that, stars were
both smaller and cooler. There were "yellow dwarfs"
(such as our sun) and very cool, dim stars called "red
dwarfs."

Evolution of Stars?

For the first time, mankind glimpsed a pattern of steady
change in the heavens. Perhaps the heavens grew old just
as the earth did; perhaps the stars had a life cycle like that
of living creatures. Perhaps there was *stellar evolution*,
evolution of the stars, just as there was evolution of life on
earth.

Russell suggested that stars were born as huge masses of
cool, thin gas that shone with a dim red heat. As they aged,
they contracted and grew hotter and hotter until they
reached a maximum temperature. They continued to con-
tract, now growing cooler and cooler, and finally became
blackened burnt-out cinders. Our sun, it seemed, was well
past middle age.

This theory, however, was too simple. Actually, at
the beginning of the twentieth century, astronomers didn't
know what made a star shine, or radiate light. In the

1880's it had been suggested that the energy for a star's radiation came from its slow contraction and that gravitational energy was converted to light. (This meshed nicely with Russell's notions.) However, such a process couldn't supply enough energy, so the idea had to be abandoned.

In the 1890's scientists had discovered that the center of the atom, its "nucleus," contained a store of energy far larger than had been imagined. In the 1930's a German-American physicist, Hans A. Bethe (BAY-tuh), worked out a scheme of nuclear reactions that could go on within the sun's interior and supply it with the energy to form light.

In these reactions, Bethe hypothesized, atoms of hydrogen (the simplest of all atoms) are converted to the slightly more complicated atoms of helium. The sun's enormous hydrogen supply has allowed it to shine for five or six billion years, with enough left over for many more billions of years. Thus, the sun is not in decline after all. It is still a young star.

Astronomers have continued to study the nature of the nuclear reactions going on within a star. As hydrogen turns to helium, they believe, the helium collects at the center as a "helium core." It continues to grow hotter as the star ages, until the helium atoms begin to interact and form still more complicated atoms. Other changes are believed to take place, too.

Tremendous Explosion

Eventually, the star's original hydrogen supply sinks below a certain level. The temperature and brightness of the star change so drastically that it leaves the main sequence. It expands enormously and sometimes begins to pulsate as its structure grows less stable.

The star may then explode. If so, virtually all its remaining "fuel" ignites at once and the star becomes exceedingly bright for a short period. Explosions such as these formed the novas observed by Hipparchus and Tycho Brahe.

In short, astronomers have developed the idea of heavenly change — which first startled Hipparchus two thousand years ago — to the point of debating how stars are born, grow, age, and die.

Astronomers can go still further. Some theorize that the universe was born in a huge explosion whose fragments are still flying apart. Each fragment is a vast galaxy of many billions of stars. Perhaps the day will come when all the galaxies will have spread out of sight, when all the stars will have exploded, and when all the universe will be dead.

Or perhaps, as some other astronomers think, the universe is constantly being reborn. Perhaps, new matter is always being formed very slowly, and from it new stars and galaxies arise as the old ones die.

Indeed, the idea of change in the heavens gives us theories not merely of stellar evolution, but of a *cosmic evolution* — a "great idea of science" almost too vast in scope to comprehend.

INDEX

Abdera, 36
Acceleration, 60
Air, 45–54
  compression of, 39–40
Air resistance, 33
Alexander the Great, 115
Alexandria, 21
Amino acids, 113
Ammonium cyanate, 107
Animals, classification of, 116–120
Archimedes, 20–23, 25–28, 31, 34
Aristotle, 26, 31, 54–57, 114–117, 121,
  129–130
Asklepios, 102
Atoms, 37
  structure of, 96–97
Axioms, 18, 24

Babylon, 4, 22
Bernoulli, Daniel, 76
Berthelot, Pierre E., 108
Berzelius Jöns J., 107
Bethe, Hans A., 135
Black, Joseph, 51
Black body, 91–92
Bohr, Niels, 96
Boltzmann, Ludwig, 77
Boyle, Robert, 39–40
Brahe, Tycho, 131
Buchner, Eduard, 111
Buffon, Georges de, 124
Bunsen, Robert Wilhelm von, 90

Caloric, 73
Carbon dioxide, 48–49, 51
Carnot, Nicholas L. S., 86–87
Catalyst, 109
Cause and effect, 99
Chaos, 47
Classes, 120
Clausius, Rudolf J. E., 87
Clock, pendulum, 35
Combustion, 49–53
Comets, 131–132
Compass, 65
Conon, 22, 24
Conservation of energy, 85
Conservation of matter, 53

Croton, 10
Cuvier, Georges, 120

Dalton, John, 41–44, 75
Darwin, Charles, 125–128
Deduction, 18
Definite proportions, law of, 41
Democritus, 36–38
Diamond, 50
Digestion, 110
Dolphins, 116

Earth, age of, 123–124
Egypt, 21
Einstein, Albert, 69, 95–96
Electric generators, 68
Electromagnetic field, 69
Electrons, 96
Energy, 81
  conservation of, 8
  quanta of, 93–94
Entropy, 88
Enzymes, 110–113
  isolation of, 112
Epicurus, 38
Epilepsy, 102, 104
Euclid, 24
Eupalinus, 22
Even numbers, 12
Evolution, 124–128
  stellar, 134–137
Experimental science, 34
Experimentation, 32

Fabricius, David, 132
Falling bodies, 31–34, 57
Faraday, Michael, 66–68
Ferments, 109–111
Fields, 68–69
Fischer, Emil, 113
Force, 60, 63
Fossils, 120

Galápagos Islands, 126
Galileo, 29–35, 57
Gases, 48–49
  kinetic theory of, 76–79
Gassendi, Pierre, 39
Genus, 118
Geometry, 19
Gods, 4
  life and, 101

138